GEORGE LINDBECK

CASCADE COMPANIONS

The Christian theological tradition provides an embarrassment of riches: from Scripture to modern scholarship, we are blessed with a vast and complex theological inheritance. And yet this feast of traditional riches is too frequently inaccessible to the general reader.

The Cascade Companions series addresses the challenge by publishing books that combine academic rigor with broad appeal and readability. They aim to introduce nonspecialist readers to that vital storehouse of authors, documents, themes, histories, arguments, and movements that comprise this heritage with brief yet compelling volumes.

GEORGE LINDBECK

A Biographical and Theological Introduction

SHAUN C. BROWN

CASCADE *Books* • Eugene, Oregon

GEORGE LINDBECK
A Biographical and Theological Introduction

Cascade Companions

Copyright © 2022 Shaun C. Brown. All rights reserved. Except for brief quotations in critical publications or reviews, no part of this book may be reproduced in any manner without prior written permission from the publisher. Write: Permissions, Wipf and Stock Publishers, 199 W. 8th Ave., Suite 3, Eugene, OR 97401.

Cascade Books
An Imprint of Wipf and Stock Publishers
199 W. 8th Ave., Suite 3
Eugene, OR 97401

www.wipfandstock.com

PAPERBACK ISBN: 978-1-5326-8873-7
HARDCOVER ISBN: 978-1-5326-8874-4
EBOOK ISBN: 978-1-5326-8875-1

Cataloguing-in-Publication data:

Names: Brown, Shaun C., author.
Title: George Lindbeck : a biographical and theological introduction / Shaun C. Brown.
Description: Eugene, OR : Cascade Books, 2022 | Series: Cascade Companions | Includes bibliographical references and index(es).
Identifiers: ISBN 978-1-5326-8873-7 (paperback) | ISBN 978-1-5326-8874-4 (hardcover) | ISBN 978-1-5326-8875-1 (Ebook)
Subjects: LCSH: Lindbeck, George A. | Israel (Christian theology). | Theology. | Church.
Classification: BR50 .B76 2022 (print) | BR50 .B76 (ebook)

TABLE OF CONTENTS

Acknowledgments vii

Introduction ix

1. Lutheran 1

2. Student 25

3. Medievalist 39

4. Observer 57

5. Ecumenist 86

6. Postliberal 107

7. Israelologist 133

Bibliography 155

Index of Names 165

Index of Subjects 167

ACKNOWLEDGMENTS

Much of the research that went into this book began while I was working on my doctoral dissertation at Wycliffe College and the University of Toronto.[1] I want to again thank my dissertation committee members—Joseph Mangina, Ephraim Radner, John Berkman, David Novak, and James Buckley—for helping me better understand George Lindbeck's life and work.

I want to thank my wife, Sherri, and our children, Adalyn, Emilia, and Ezra, for supporting me as I worked on this project.

I also want to thank Kris Lindbeck, Bruce Marshall, and Michael Root for their willingness to answer some of my questions. Finally, I want to thank Justus Hunter, Stephen Lawson, and John Nugent for their willingness to read the first draft of this project, as well as Charlie Collier and the team at Wipf and Stock. Each of them offered suggestions and comments that helped improve the final product. Any problems that remain are the fault of the author.

---

1. It has since been published as Brown, *George Lindbeck*.

INTRODUCTION

ON MORE THAN ONE occasion while writing my dissertation, I would be in a library at the University of Toronto tracking down journal articles or chapters in books, and I would bump into another doctoral student. They would ask, "What are you working on?" I would tell them that I am writing my dissertation on George Lindbeck (1923–2018), the noted American Lutheran historical theologian and ecumenist. They would then say something along the lines of, "That's interesting, but how do you write a dissertation on someone who only wrote one book?"

Many have read his most influential work, *The Nature of Doctrine*, which Karen Kilby refers to as "probably the most significant work of American theology in a generation, if not a century,"[1] and Bruce Marshall contends "became the most widely read and debated theological treatise of the last fifty years."[2] Despite this, they have read little else of his corpus. In a way, that makes sense. Lindbeck wrote few complete books. Most of his writing is scattered among various journals, multi-author volumes, and

---

1. Kilby, "Ecumenical Generosity," 6.
2. Marshall, "Discovering Agreement," 10.

Introduction

ecumenical statements, so few have taken the time to read these writings.[3]

To understand Lindbeck's project, however, one must not only know about his writings. Lindbeck led a fascinating life, from his upbringing in China to his participation as an observer at the Second Vatican Council, from his studies at Yale, Toronto, Paris, and Tübingen to his participation in Lutheran-Catholic dialogues. These experiences brought Lindbeck into contact with many of the most significant theologians and ecclesiastical leaders of the twentieth century, and one cannot understand his work apart these experiences. As Frederick Christian Bauerschmidt argues, "When studying some theologians, it seems crucial to understand their lives in order to understand their thought."[4]

I cannot cover everything within these pages, but I hope, in this brief volume, to remedy this situation by providing (1) a context for understanding *The Nature of Doctrine*, (2) a corrective to misreadings of Lindbeck's work, (3) an introduction to his broader corpus, and (4) some possible ways in which Lindbeck's work can contribute to future ecumenical discussion and to Christian theological practice more broadly. Most of all, I hope that these chapters will lead people to read Lindbeck's own writings.

There are various ways that someone could introduce Lindbeck's life and work. For instance, in the introduction to *The Church in a Postliberal Age*, James J. Buckley introduces Lindbeck by using three categories: evangelical, catholic, and postliberal. Buckley notes that Lindbeck

---

3. We are most fortunate that one of his students, James Buckley (1947–), collected some of his most important essays and edited *The Church in a Postliberal Age* (Eerdmans, 2002), but most of his writing is still difficult to access.

4. Bauerschmidt, *Holy Teaching*, 12.

Introduction

is, first and foremost, a Christian, and specifically, an Evangelical Lutheran. Second, Lindbeck is committed to the unity of the one, holy, catholic, and apostolic church; an ecumenist who was an observer at the Second Vatican Council and participant in Lutheran-Catholic dialogue. Third, Lindbeck cast a vision for a "postliberal" theology—a theology that envisioned religions as analogous to cultures and languages. Buckley notes that he then "applies and extends this postliberal theology" in his work on the church as Israel.[5]

This book will follow a slightly different organization but will utilize each of the three categories used by Buckley. Each chapter will focus on a role or aspect of Lindbeck's life and thought. It will begin by discussing Lindbeck's Lutheran background and his understanding of Luther and the Lutheran Reformation of the sixteenth century. Chapter 2 will consider Lindbeck's studies in New Haven, Toronto, and Paris, and the influence of his teachers upon his thought. Chapter 3 will focus upon Lindbeck's work as a medievalist, especially his understanding of Thomas Aquinas. Chapter 4 will examine Lindbeck's work as an observer at the Second Vatican Council and his later reflections upon the council's significance. Chapter 5 will discuss Lindbeck's understanding of ecumenical dialogue and, in particular, his work on the doctrine of justification. Chapter 6 provides a reading of *The Nature of Doctrine* and introduces Lindbeck's understanding of postliberal theology. Chapter 7 concludes the volume with a treatment of Lindbeck's later work upon the church as "Israel-like" or "as Israel."[6] Some of these roles, such as his denominational

5. Buckley, "Introduction," xii–xiii.

6. Among the gaping holes in my account is that I do not provide a chapter on Lindbeck's role as a teacher. Several of his former students speak about his teaching style in their honorariums upon his

affiliation, continued throughout his life, while some others, like his service as a Lutheran observer at the Second Vatican Council, will cover an episode in his life that changed the trajectory of his life and career.

---

death. See Casarella, "Mr. Lindbeck," 369–75; Congrove, "Fides," 29; Kilby, "Ecumenical Generosity," 8; Mangina, "Charitable Reading," 27–28; Marshall, "Discovering Agreement," 11; Radner, "Quiet," 22; Reno, "George Lindbeck," 66–68; Root, "Humble and Focused," 29. Marshall says, "He was, by a long shot, the best teacher I ever had."

1

LUTHERAN

IT MIGHT SEEM ODD to begin a book about a noted ecumenist, a person committed to church unity, with a chapter on his denominational background. If one is so committed to the unity of the church, should she not eschew loyalty to a Christian sect in order to embrace the universal church? As Lindbeck himself says, "What the good God is doing to the church, it seems to me, is destroying us bit by bit. And destroying each denomination's identity is precisely the way in which we'll have to be united."[1] Lindbeck argues, however, that one can only participate in ecumenism by being rooted in their own tradition. While one can find fellowship with other Christians in a shared love of God revealed in Jesus Christ, he says, "if you are going to be really ecumenical, you are going to have to know your own tradition and love it to its depths."[2] Or as he says elsewhere, paraphrasing C. S. Lewis through Yves Congar, "It is important for divided Christians to help one another live faithfully the Christian

1. Wright, "Israel," 118.
2. Wright, "Israel," 118.

life of their own confession, because it is thus that they draw spiritually closest to one another."[3]

So, in order to understand Lindbeck's life and writings, one must come to understand Lindbeck as a distinctly Lutheran theologian. One of Lindbeck's former students, Cyril O'Regan (1952–), says that while many looked to Lindbeck as the "quintessential ecumenical theologian," O'Regan saw Lindbeck as the "quintessential Lutheran theologian."[4] This chapter alone cannot exhaustively treat what it means for Lindbeck to be a Lutheran. In fact, there is a sense in which this entire book is an introduction to Lindbeck as a Lutheran theologian, for he was a Lutheran observer at the Second Vatican Council, a Lutheran participant in ecumenical dialogues, and offered an ecumenical, yet Lutheran, understanding of the relation of the churches to the church. This chapter will accomplish a simpler task: exploring Lindbeck's understanding of the Lutheran tradition and of Martin Luther (1483–1546).

YOUTH

George Arthur Lindbeck was born on March 10, 1923, in Luoyang, China, the fourth and youngest child of Swedish-American Lutheran missionaries. Though Loyang had been the imperial capital of China off and on prior to AD 700, it was in many ways a pre-modern city, lacking electricity or running water. He spent the first seventeen years of his life there.[5] Though Lindbeck did not do much academic reflection on China or Confucianism in his later years, he

3. Lindbeck, "Paris," 396.

4. O'Regan, "Quintessential," 25. O'Regan says, "While I understood and appreciated the first, the latter was more important to me, but perhaps for more than the usual reasons."

5. Lindbeck, "Confession and Community," 392.

Lutheran

speaks very highly of the Chinese people and their culture and argues this time left lasting marks upon his thought. First, he came to see that "the communal shapes us more than we shape ourselves." Second, humans, even those separated by place and time, are more alike than they are different. Third, despite these similarities, cultural and linguistic differences can "sometimes make communication almost though not entirely impossible." Fourth, and most important from Lindbeck's perspective, "book-sustained continuities of community-creating thought and practice can survive thousands of years of political, social, economic and even linguistic upheaval."[6] He also argues that his own sense of unease with Christendom and cultural Christianity likely came from his time living in China.[7]

There were a variety of Protestant missionaries in China at the time, from high-church Anglicans to Pentecostals, most of them from English-speaking countries. He notes that despite these diverse denominational backgrounds, the missionaries got along well with one another. The adults around him were aware of ecumenism and the ecumenical movement, but most of them were theologically conservative and viewed the movement, as well as modernism, with suspicion. They set up comity arrangements in order to prevent "sheep-stealing" between the various Christian groups, and Lindbeck says, "This was an essential precondition for the mutual goodwill that made possible much cooperation, shared worship, and even intercommunion."[8]

A kind of pan-Protestant interdenominationalism pervaded the missionary culture as well as the boarding

6. Lindbeck, "Performing the Faith," 28.

7. Lindbeck, "Confession and Community," 392.

8. Lindbeck, "Paris," 390. He notes, however, that some Anglicans and Lutherans may have quietly not participated in intercommunion.

school that he and his siblings attended. Lindbeck argues that while Christians of different backgrounds attended this school, it was "not in the least ecumenical, and that has greatly influenced my ecumenism. I have, in short, rebelled against it."[9] In one sense, the missionaries and the boarding school had a sense of Christian unity. Justification by faith alone was shared by both "Baptist conversionist evangelicals" and "Lutheran sacramental pietists." In another sense, they were all committed to their own denominational theology and practice. Lindbeck remembers, for example, arguing with Baptists about infant baptism and baptismal regeneration. Despite these disagreements, he and his fellow classmates, as well as most of the adults in their lives, largely saw invisible unity in Christ as sufficient.[10]

Roman Catholics were largely absent from Lindbeck's upbringing in Asia. He did have some cousins who were Catholic, children of his mother's brother. He remembers visiting them as a child while his parents were on furlough. He did not realize until later that they were a part of the church that persecuted Luther and slaughtered the Christians that he read about in Foxe's *Book of Martyrs*.[11] While he did not deny that some Catholics might be genuine Christians, like Fr. Damien and St. Francis, he shared the suspicions of Catholicism that many of the adults in his life had:

> I learned to think of the Roman Catholic Church as a vast conspiracy dominating the consciences of its members, in which the priests monopolized and manipulated the means of

---

9. Lindbeck, "Paris," 389. Lindbeck says that because of illness, he did not go to the boarding school until he was twelve. See Lindbeck, "Confession and Community," 492.

10. Lindbeck, "Paris," 390.

11. Lindbeck, "Confession and Community," 493.

> grace and thus denied that Christ is the "sole mediator" between human beings and God—a phrase familiar to us already by grade school. We were also taught that the papists, as we heard them called, affirmed that salvation was at least partly earned through supposedly meritorious works rather than through faith in Jesus Christ alone. Moreover, the hierarchy encouraged all sorts of superstitious beliefs and practices in order to keep control of the people, especially in unenlightened places such as Spain and Latin America.[12]

Protestants and Catholics rarely met in China. To this day Protestant and Catholic Christians use different names to refer to God, and the Chinese government continues to treat them as two separate religions.

Lindbeck, like most Lutherans over the last five centuries, memorized Luther's Small Catechism as a part of his catechetical instruction.[13] Despite this, his parents and other Lutherans he knew often downplayed their differences from the Protestant evangelicals around them. He says, "This was easy for them, for they were for the most part pietists of biblicistic and conversionist proclivities, but it confused me."[14] He knew that Lutherans were different from other Protestants, but other than the disagreements over issues like infant baptism, he did not know in what way.

While in high school, he came to have more of an understanding of his Lutheran identity through a new headmaster at his school, Pastor Albue, who "alerted me to the possibility of an unambiguously confessional Lutheranism

12. Lindbeck, "Paris," 392.
13. Lindbeck, "Paris," 390.
14. Lindbeck, "Confession and Community," 494.

that was devout but not pietistic, and quite unreticent about baptismal regeneration and the real presence." Others he came to know during this time, like a Norwegian missionary scholar named K. L. Reichelt (1933–2016), helped further solidify this understanding of Lutheranism. Lindbeck says, "Through such influences, I began to opt for a Reformation Christianity self-consciously opposed to modern Protestantism in both its conservative and liberal forms. Its starting point is neither biblicistic nor experientialist, and certainly not individualistic, but dogmatic: it commences with the historic Christian communal confession of faith in Christ."[15]

CORRECTIVE VIEW OF THE REFORMATION

As an adult, Lindbeck came even further under the influence of confessional Lutherans. He notes four as having a great influence on him: Danish theologian Kristen E. Skydsgaard (1902–1990), Germans Peter Brunner (1900–1981) and Edmund Schlink (1903–1984), and American Arthur Carl Piepkorn (1907–1973). From them, he came to see the Lutheran Reformation as "a reform movement within the Catholic Church of the West."[16] He calls this the *corrective* view of the Reformation.[17] The earliest Reformers had no intention of starting a new church. They sought, instead, to reform the church of Rome. When they later began to ordain ministers outside of apostolic tradition, they did so

15. Lindbeck, "Confession and Community," 494.

16. Lindbeck, "Confession and Community," 494. Lindbeck includes the qualification "West" here because, as he notes elsewhere, the earliest Reformers recognized that "the Orthodox in the East had an equal claim to catholicity and apostolicity" (Lindbeck, "A Protestant View," 244).

17. Granfield, "George Lindbeck," 153–55.

Lutheran

as an emergency measure until they could reunite with the church in the West and bring about its reform:

> These are familiar historical facts which have often been noted in recent years, but it is difficult for us to remember their significance. The Catholic Church was for the early Protestants the one and only church, it was their home church, it was their ecclesiastical homeland—but it was under enemy occupation. The government had become tyrannical. It drove out not only those who would reform it, but even those who asked for nothing more than the freedom to preach the gospel. There was nothing to do except to form a government, an ecclesiastical order, in exile. But the Reformers at first no more thought of this as a new, a second church than De Gaulle thought of his war-time regime as a replacement, a substitute for France . . . Their claim was not that they represented the only legitimate regime, but that theirs was a legitimate interim order until such time as reforms made it possible to rejoin the homeland.[18]

Lindbeck thus argues that it is Lutheranism, rather than Anglicanism, that served as a bridge between Protestantism and Catholicism.[19]

Protestants, however, soon stopped seeing the Roman Catholic Church as their homeland. Instead of seeing themselves as exiles wanting to return home, they soon came to see the Roman Catholic Church as Egypt and their

---

18. Lindbeck, "A Protestant View," 244–45.

19. Lindbeck, "The Crucial Role," 8. He says, however, "That's not meant as a putdown. Anglicans can and do serve bridging functions—for example between East and West—that Lutherans are simply incapable of" (8–9).

new churches as the Promised Land.[20] Lindbeck calls this the *constitutive* view of the Reformation, and he argues that it can be observed in second-generation reformers like John Calvin (1509–1564), as well as later figures in the Lutheran tradition.

CONFESSIONS AND CONFESSIONAL SUBSCRIPTION

Each Christian group is held together by distinctive emphases. For example, Anglicans are held together by the Book of Common Prayer, Presbyterians by shared polity, Orthodox by tradition, and Roman Catholics by the papacy. Lindbeck argues that Lutherans are held together by their confessions. He writes, "More than any other major Christian communion, our identity and unity are dependent on our confessions."[21] He points to Alasdair MacIntyre's definition of a tradition as an "argument extended through time"[22] and says that within Lutheranism, the arguments have largely been over how to understand their confessions. While he acknowledges that confessions can be "sinfully misused," he argues that "they can also be means God uses to mobilize the commitments and energies of believers in communally effective and constructive ways."[23] This does not mean Lindbeck believes confessions supersede or replace Scripture. They are instead in service of Scripture, which is the *norma*

20. Lindbeck, "A Protestant View," 245. See also Lindbeck, "Confessional Subscription," 317.

21. Lindbeck, "Confessional Faithfulness," 61. Lindbeck covers much of this same material in Lindbeck, "Ecumenical Directions," 118–23.

22. Macintyre, *Whose Justice?*, 12.

23. Lindbeck, "Confessional Faithfulness," 61.

normans non normata ("the norming norm that cannot be normed"). The confessions function similarly to the ancient *regula fidei* ("rule of faith"), which developed to ensure that the Bible is read "as testimony to and from the creator God whose Word enfleshed is Jesus Christ."[24] The Confessions' authority must be understood as "tertiary and historically conditioned, yet . . . hermeneutically absolute for those who subscribe to them."[25]

Lindbeck argues that other than the early Christian creeds, the Augsburg Confession is "the most authoritative of the Lutheran symbols of faith," for the others, like Luther's catechisms, are "pastoral applications . . . or interpretations to fit later circumstances."[26] A particularly important aspect of Augsburg is its ecumenical intent. Augsburg was written in an attempt to prevent schism within the Catholic Church of the West. Lindbeck sees Augsburg as a precedent and argues that it should be reaffirmed.[27] He calls those in his camp "movement" Lutherans. Those who disagree with him and his camp and do not believe Lutherans should treat Augsburg as a precedent for the contemporary church, he calls "denominational church" Lutherans.[28] His distinction between movement and denominational Lutherans corresponds to his

---

24. Lindbeck, "Confessional Subscription," 319.

25. Lindbeck, "Confessional Subscription," 319.

26. Lindbeck, "Confessional Faithfulness," 61.

27. Lindbeck participated in a dialogue over whether the contemporary Roman Catholic Church could come to recognize Augsburg. See Lindbeck and Vajta, "The Augsburg Confession," 81–94.

28. Lindbeck, "Confessional Faithfulness," 62. Of course, there are constitutive or denominational Lutherans who are also confessionalists.

distinction between a corrective and constitutive view of the Reformation.[29]

The Lutheran confessions, like Augsburg, point to an emphasis upon the "solas" as the "theological center" of the Reformation heritage. Lindbeck says that there are three interconnected solas: *solus Christus*, *sola fides* (in which he includes *sola gratia*), and *sola Scriptura*.[30] He notes, too, that Luther and Calvin, and to a certain extent Ulrich Zwingli (1484–1531), understood these solas in almost identical ways: "For them the heart of the Christian gospel and the Christian life is salvation by grace and faith alone in Christ alone as witnessed to by Scripture alone."[31] These three solas were not only liberating for individual Christians, but for the church at large. They provide a consensus on how Scripture should "function as a truly effective communal authority, as both a judge of the church and a creator of unity."[32]

He says that movement Lutherans, like himself, first, hold to "a generally catholic type of ecclesiology which stresses the importance of the visible unity and continuity of the church."[33] Lindbeck argues that the Reformation emphasis upon the solas did not *replace* the previous tradition, but instead provided a corrective that stands in

29. Lindbeck notes that some others within his own camp prefer the term "evangelical catholics," but Gerhard Forde has also noted that this term is used by some who are either not Lutherans or not confessionalists. Therefore, Lindbeck sticks with the terms "movement" or "'corrective' confessionalists" (Lindbeck, "Confessional Faithfulness," 63).

30. Lindbeck, "The Reformation Heritage," 484. He notes here that Calvin would also point to a fourth sola, "to the glory of God alone," but Lindbeck does not see this as a disagreement (485).

31. Lindbeck, "The Reformation Heritage," 484.

32. Lindbeck, "The Reformation Heritage," 484.

33. Lindbeck, "Confessional Faithfulness," 63.

continuity with the catholic tradition. So instead of seeing the Reformation emphasis upon justification by faith as constitutive of a new type of Christianity, movement Lutherans argue that every doctrine is susceptible to abuse and corruption, and therefore may be in need of reform:

> There is no room for the ecclesiological triumphalism of a *theologia gloria* on the Reformation side any more than on the Roman one. The marks of the church—its oneness, holiness, catholicity and apostolicity—are hidden under their contraries (*sub contrario*, as Luther would say). Yet visible unity and continuity are important, and their restoration wherever there is freedom for the gospel is imperative.[34]

Second, movement Lutherans see the Lutheran tradition as "a movement of confessional renewal within the Catholic Church of the West which has been unjustly but, it is hoped, temporarily expelled from the Roman communion."[35] He and other movement Lutherans thus call upon the Lutheran tradition to become what it initially sought to be: "an agent of evangelical renewal within rather than outside the ancient churches of the West (and also East) which comprise the great majority of Christians."[36] He holds out hope that if this were to happen, that it would have a great consequence not only for Lutherans, but for all Christians, saying, "The Lutheran Confessions do not simply introduce enriching variety into the ecumenical chorus, but as [Eric W.] Gritsch [1931–2012] and [Robert] Jenson [1930–2017] put it, they propose a dogma for all Christians, namely, that the triune God whose Word

---

34. Lindbeck, "Confessional Faithfulness," 63.
35. Lindbeck, "Confessional Faithfulness," 63.
36. Lindbeck, "Confessional Faithfulness," 63.

became flesh in Jesus Christ justifies sinners *sola gratia* and *sola fide*."[37]

Lindbeck says, "The failure to take sufficient account of communal tradition results, so it can be said, in a neglect of the Old Testament sense of the church as God's chosen people which remains elect even when faithless and which, just because it is chosen, can become worse than the heathen when it refuses to heed God's word."[38] While he agrees with the Lutheran tradition that justification by faith alone is the doctrine on which the church stands or falls, he argues that all "gospel treasures" are held and communicated in history within the *corpus mixtum*, the mixed body that is the church on earth. He argues that those who hold to a constitutive view of the Reformation often have a docetic understanding of the church, and therefore have difficulty recognizing the continuity of the church and the search for visible Christian unity. Lindbeck concludes:

> To the degree that we begin thinking of ourselves as a reform movement within the Catholic Church of the West, we are not repudiating our original heritage, but rather we are regaining or reaffirming what we were at the beginning. Then our reality will come to correspond more closely to what we officially profess to be. Then our communal identity will succeed in becoming what our founding document, the Augsburg Confession, says that we want to be—both Protestant, thoroughly devoted to the centrality of justification by faith, and at the same time Catholic, in communion with the unbroken structures of the Western Church. If this is to be done, it must be done by Lutherans or else it will be done by no one. We were the first to

---

37. Lindbeck, "Confessional Subscription," 319.
38. Lindbeck, "Confessional Faithfulness," 65.

make the break. And so in the logic of history—sometimes history does have logic as well as accidents—if the breach is to be healed, we must be the ones who heal it.[39]

MARTIN LUTHER

Lindbeck claims that he is not a "professional Luther scholar," for he was trained as a medievalist and has used that training to become an expert in contemporary Roman Catholicism.[40] Lindbeck is, however, being somewhat modest here. He translated Luther[41] and also wrote several scholarly essays that engage Luther. Luther and Thomas Aquinas were the two theologians that he engaged with the most.[42] He admits that "as it often happens to those of Lutheran upbringing, the Reformer keeps constantly tugging at my attention."[43]

Luther as Pastor and Catechist

In his essay, "Martin Luther and the Rabbinic Mind," Lindbeck offers a somewhat unique depiction of Luther. He notes that most scholarly historical and theological treatments focus on Luther as a "theological controversialist." Lindbeck instead tries to engage Luther not from the perspective of scholars, but from a parishioner's point of view: "Unlike scholars, ordinary folk deeply socialized

---

39. Lindbeck, "The Crucial Role," 9. Lindbeck also argues that Lutherans have a particularly important role to play in North America.
40. Lindbeck, "Erikson's Young Man Luther," 210.
41. Luther, "*Contra Latomus.*"
42. Lindbeck, "Forward," xxxi.
43. Lindbeck, "Modernity," 1.

into the normative versions of Luther's Reformation knew him chiefly as pastor and catechist, not theological controversialist. I believe their view comes closer to the original Luther than do most scholarly reconstructions, including Lutheran ones."[44] He makes this case, in part, by pointing to the table of contents from Luther's collected works, the *Weimar Ausgabe*. He notes that the majority of Luther's writings are "pastorally-oriented sermons, commentaries, table talk, letters and, of course, the catechisms"[45]

While conceding that Luther was also a theological controversialist *par excellence*, Lindbeck argues that his most influential works were not these controversial writings, but his Large and Small Catechisms and his German translation of the Bible. In Lindbeck's estimation, "The Catechisms provide the most authoritative normative description of Reformation Christianity as a religion of the population at large."[46] Unlike in Luther's controversial writings, the Catechisms do not explicitly mention justification by faith alone, total depravity, predestination, or the relation of law and gospel. On this last issue, Lindbeck argues, "There is thus little or no hint of the antinomian devaluation of good works, Manichaeism and determinism, which Luther's opponents (as well as some of his purported followers) deduced, to his dismay, from systematic reconstruals of his theology."[47] There is not, within the Catechisms, an opposition between beliefs and ethics, individual and community, experience and worship rites. Lindbeck says, "According to this depiction, Luther

44. Lindbeck, "Martin Luther," 142.

45. Lindbeck, "Martin Luther," 142.

46. Lindbeck, "Martin Luther," 143.

47. Lindbeck, "Martin Luther," 143. See also Lindbeck, "Luther on Law," 270–74.

offered his theological ideas only in the context of his recommendations for practice."[48]

Despite Luther's anti-Judaism and anti-Semitism, Lindbeck concludes that there are similarities between Luther's treatment of the Christian faith and tradition in the Catechisms and rabbinic Judaism. For example, Luther organized the Catechisms around five topics: Ten Commandments, Apostles' Creed, Lord's Prayer, Baptism, and the Lord's Supper. Lindbeck argues that these five topics correspond to five foci in rabbinic catechetical writing: *torah* (law, instruction), *shema* (Deut 6:4–5), the *amidah* (a central prayer in the Jewish liturgy), circumcision, and the Passover *seder*. Lindbeck notes that rabbi Max Kadushin (1895–1980) sees these five topics as "organically related." Lindbeck expounds upon this by saying, "Decalogue, creed, prayer, and sacraments is each important in its own right, yet no one of them can authentically exist without all the others, and there is no logically deductive or formally inferential relation of subordination or superordination between them."[49]

Luther on the Creed

Luther also referred to the Creed as "*historia historiarum*, 'the story of stories.'"[50] He saw the Creed as "a summary of the gospel, and the gospel, in turn, is narrative: it proclaims God's gracious dealings with humankind in creation, the coming of Jesus Christ (the climactic part of the story) and the gathering of a people, the church, through the

---

48. Lindbeck, "Martin Luther," 141.

49. Lindbeck, "Martin Luther," 144.

50. Lindbeck, "Martin Luther," 145. Lindbeck notes that Luther also called the Lord's Prayer the "*oratio orationum* and baptism and the eucharist "*ceremonia ceremoniarum*."

Holy Spirit."[51] The Creed only provides a brief summary of the story, but Luther argues that this is acceptable because the sermons heard throughout the year fill in the gaps. Lindbeck argues that Luther's sermons functioned like haggadic midrash,[52] expounding upon the creedal narrative.[53]

For Luther, dogmas "are implied by the creedal narratives."[54] And not only that, they are truth claims. Dogmas, however, are first communicated to us in stories. The stories are primary for Luther. When Christians come to understand from these stories how God has acted *pro me*, they "become one's own story, they elicit the fear, love, and trust of God above all things which, according to Luther,

---

51. Lindbeck, "Martin Luther," 145.

52. Haggadah refers to nonprescriptive or narrative texts in Scripture, as well as to the narrative of the exodus from Egypt that Jews retell during the Passover *seder*. Donald McKim defines midrash as "Commentary and explanatory notes on the Scriptures produced by Jewish sages from the period of the Babylonian exile (5th century BCE) until c. 1200 CE" (McKim, *The Westminster Dictionary*, 198). Wilda Gafney says that traditional midrash not only involves exegesis or close reading of a biblical text, but "is also mystical, imaginative, revelatory, and, above all, religious. Midrash interprets not only the text before the reader, but also the text behind and beyond the text and the text between the lines of the text. In rabbinic thinking, each letter and the spaces between the letters are available for interpretive work. Midrash is rarely comprehensive and occasionally contradictory, raising as many questions as it answers" (Gafney, *Womanist Midrash*, 4–5).

53. Lindbeck notes, however, that Luther largely neglects narratives about the formation of Israel as a people and does not discuss the Exodus narrative in the Catechisms and rarely discusses it elsewhere in his corpus. He says, "The stories which interested Luther, in contrast, were those he could expand into *exempla* for the lives of the saints (that is, 'sinners justified by faith') in all times and places" (Lindbeck, "Martin Luther," 146n14). The narratives that Luther neglects are the ones Lindbeck privileges. See chapter 7.

54. Lindbeck, "Martin Luther," 146.

is the sum and substance of the first commandments and without which we cannot rightly obey any of the others."[55] Dogmas then play a servant role, providing aid in interpreting the stories that shape the lives of Christians. Also, these dogmas or doctrines lose their meaning when they are "abstracted from their narrative and practical settings."[56] Lindbeck likens Luther's perspective on the role of doctrines to his own discussion of doctrines as rules in *The Nature of Doctrine*.[57]

Luther on the Decalogue

Luther referred to the Ten Commandments or Decalogue as "*doctrina doctrinarum*, 'the teaching of teachings.'"[58] This is a different perspective than one typically hears of the Ten Commandments, and it also differs from how people typically understand Luther's own perspective on the law. Luther is generally seen, perhaps more than any other major figure in the Christian tradition, to strengthen the Pauline distinction between law and gospel. Lindbeck argues that this is based on Luther's controversial writings in which he focuses upon the law as a tyrant and an accuser. In response to these aspects of the law, Luther emphasizes Christian freedom from the law and the grace and forgiveness of Jesus Christ. Lindbeck says, "Apart from the reference to Christ, there is perhaps nothing in this account which a rabbi would not be able to say of the law as it applies to the wicked, but Luther goes on paradoxically to insist that the law coerces and accuses the righteous just as it does the wicked, and yet is also totally abolished for

   55. Lindbeck, "Martin Luther," 147.
   56. Lindbeck, "Martin Luther," 148.
   57. Lindbeck, "Martin Luther," 148–49n27.
   58. Lindbeck, "Martin Luther," 145.

them."[59] According to Luther, that is because those who are in Christ are "simultaneously wholly just and wholly sinners, *simul totus justus et totus peccator.*"[60]

Later Lutherans like Søren Kierkegaard (1813–1855) and Dietrich Bonhoeffer (1906–1945) expressed concern that the Lutheran emphasis upon liberation from the law has made Christianity into a religion of "cheap grace." There has at times been an assumption, if not a critique, that Luther is an antinomian. If this is indeed the case, then Luther's understanding of the law would be completely unrabbinic: "There is no talk of the law as a welcome guide, a light to the feet and a lamp to the path (Ps. 119:105), and there appear to be no Christian analogues to the rabbis' delight in *halakhah.*"[61]

Lindbeck notes, however, that Luther's Catechisms provide a much different picture:

> The theological polemic against the law is absent, and Luther meditates on the commandments at length and not without pleasure. They come first, and their exposition in the Large Catechism goes on for twenty-five thousand words: nearly half of the entire Catechism and close to five times as long as his comments on the creed, *historia*. The proportions in the Small Catechism are similar if one adds to the decalogue the appendices on religious practice and household duties. Thus, the Luther of the Catechisms is, at least

---

59. Lindbeck, "Martin Luther," 149.

60. Lindbeck, "Martin Luther," 150.

61. Lindbeck, "Martin Luther," 150. McKim defines *halakah* as, "The body of teaching that grew up in Jewish law that sought to apply the law to all situations of life and to give instruction. It contrasts with haggadah" (McKim, *The Westminster Dictionary*, 142).

> quantitatively, primarily a halakhist, just as were the rabbis of the Talmud.[62]

Luther does not, in the Catechisms, refer to the Decalogue as "law," but rather, as *doctrina*: "teaching" or "instruction." He uses the term "law" to refer to human (especially papal) "enactments ... which illicitly claim divine sanction."[63]

In addition to treating the Decalogue as doctrine, Luther treats it as a guide for human life. In fact, he argues that "anyone who knows the Ten Commandments perfectly knows the entire scriptures."[64] The commands help us know God's will for our lives. And Luther argues that just because we are incapable of perfectly fulfilling the commands of God does not mean we should not try to obey. Luther warned about the threats of punishment for those who disobey.

Luther saw the Ten Commandments as a treasure, and this impacted his own practice. In his recommendations for morning and evening prayer in the Small Catechism, Luther suggests that alongside reciting the Creed and the Lord's Prayer that people sing a hymn—in particular, a hymn on the Ten Commandments.[65] Elsewhere, in a letter to Peter Beskendorf, Luther says that alongside praying through a psalm, the Creed, and the Lord's Prayer, that he prays through the Ten Commandments in order to guard himself from sin. In this context, he cites Psalm 1: "Blessed is he who meditates upon his law day and night."[66] He prays through the Commandments by breaking down each one into four parts: "I think of each commandment

---

62. Lindbeck, "Martin Luther," 151.
63. Lindbeck, "Martin Luther," 152.
64. Lindbeck, "Martin Luther," 152.
65. Luther, "Small Catechism," 352–53.
66. Luther, "A Practical Way," 34.

as, first, instruction, which is really what the Lord God demands of me so earnestly. Secondly, I turn it into a thanksgiving; third, a confession, and fourth a prayer."[67]

Lindbeck says, "For the pastoral and catechetical Luther, as for the rabbis, the commandments—albeit 10 and not 613—provide an all-embracing order for human existence."[68] Because of this, Luther's approach to justification by faith and to the law is anything but antinomian. He did not oppose God's commandments, but criticized treating them as simply instrumental, utilizing them to seek God's favor, congratulating oneself for a job well done, and, worst of all, attempting to earn salvation. Obedience to the commands of God is a good in and of itself, apart from any reward or increase in virtue.[69] Lindbeck argues that as the church increasingly becomes a minority within North America, "Christianity will need to follow the historic, mainstream practice of seeking guidance, not primarily from the Sermon on the Mount in isolation from the Tanakh, nor from the spirits of the *Zeitgeist*, but from the Decalogue interpreted from the New Testament."[70]

---

67. Luther, "A Practical Way," 36.

68. Lindbeck, "Martin Luther," 155. Lindbeck also says here that the rabbis have a counterpart for Luther's doctrine of justification by faith: "that God's goodness toward his people comes before their obedience to him. God's goodness alone makes possible acceptance of his kingship, *malkhut shamayim*, and obedience to his commandments" (155).

69. Lindbeck, "Martin Luther," 157–59. See also Lindbeck, "The Gospel's Uniqueness," 446. Though, Lindbeck argues, it is because obedience is a good in and of itself that virtue may also arise through obedience.

70. Lindbeck, "Martin Luther," 164.

Lindbeck concludes that for Luther, Christianity was "a *halakhically* structured and *aggadically*[71] constituted communal tradition which has no single, describable core meaning or essence any more than does a language or culture."[72] So while the anti-Judaism in Luther's thought is "inexcusable," Lindbeck admits, "this anti-Judaism need not be seen as structurally embedded in Luther's thought."[73]

What we also see from Lindbeck's discussion of Luther is that his own emphasis upon narrative(s) did not arise only out of some "narrative turn" in twentieth century philosophy and theology, but from his own Lutheran background. For Luther says, "The gospel is a story about Christ, God's and David's Son, who died and was raised and is established as Lord. This is the gospel in a nutshell."[74] One can also see that Lindbeck's own emphasis upon the Christian faith as one not only believed, but lived and practiced in concrete communities, arises from his own formation in the Lutheran tradition.

CONCLUSION: THE FUTURE OF LUTHERANISM

Lindbeck argues that there are four possible directions for Lutheranism in North America. The first and fourth emphasize Lutheran distinctives, while the second and third are "assimilationist" in different ways.[75] First, it could seek to repristinate the past. He sees this option as the "least feasible" because "Ethnic enclaves have largely disappeared, thus there is neither sociological or normative

---

71. Lindbeck connects *aggadah* with narrative and *historia*, "history" (Lindbeck, "Martin Luther," 142, 152).

72. Lindbeck, "Martin Luther," 161.

73. Lindbeck, "Martin Luther," 162.

74. Luther, "A Brief Instruction," 72.

75. Lindbeck, "Lutheranism," 46.

confessional support for reghettoization."[76] Second, some Lutherans find themselves drawn to conservative evangelicalism due to its biblicism, but Lindbeck does not entertain this possibility because its nonsacramentalism chafes against the Lutheran tradition. Third, Lutheranism can move closer to the liberal Protestant tendency to "downgrade historic doctrines," which would lead to "an even more decisive abandonment of Lutheran identity."[77] Some find this approach attractive, but Lindbeck argues that for those who seek to remain active in service to the church, it is not a live option.

This leaves the fourth option, which he calls "Catholic rapprochement." This approach seeks to be "evangelical without being conversionist; sacramental, confessional, and liturgical without being Romanist; and non-puritanic and non-fundamentalist without being liberal or secularized."[78] As discussed previously in this chapter, this viewpoint sees Lutheranism as a reform movement within the church catholic. This approach involves a retrieval of the self-understanding of the earliest reformers and maintains an emphasis upon Lutheran distinctives. He acknowledges that this approach comes with challenges. While he argues for a corrective view of the Reformation, many Lutherans have come to hold to a constitutive view of the Reformation. They have come to understand themselves in opposition to Rome. Changes will have to come for Lutherans, as well as the Roman Catholic Church, in order for Lutherans to more widely embrace this approach. But these practical difficulties, he argues,

---

76. Lindbeck, "Lutheran Churches," 442.
77. Lindbeck, "Lutheran Churches," 442.
78. Lindbeck, "Lutheranism," 45.

Lutheran

are not a reason for inaction, but only for patience and wisdom. Catholic rapprochement should not be pushed in such a way as to impede the communication of the gospel to those who are traditionally Lutheran; and the emphasis in addressing those who are from non-Lutheran backgrounds should be on the combination of evangelical and catholic elements without emphasizing that this is peculiarly Lutheran.[79]

Discussion Questions:

1. Is Lindbeck correct that one can only be engaged ecumenically from a situatedness within a tradition?
2. Given that most Protestant traditions affirm a constitutive view of the Reformation or of their own tradition, is it possible for them to recapture or embrace a corrective view of the Reformation?
3. Lindbeck argues that confessions hold the Lutheran tradition together. What distinctives hold your own tradition together? In what way are they in service to the church's reading of Scripture?
4. Luther is often read primarily as a theological controversialist. Does Lindbeck make a sufficient case for instead seeing his pastoral and catechetical works as primary instead?
5. Contemporary readers often find Luther's language about the Jews deeply offensive. Lindbeck, however, sees connections between Luther's thought and aspects of rabbinic exegesis and concludes that "this anti-Judaism need not be seen as structurally

---

79. Lindbeck, "Lutheran Churches," 443.

embedded in Luther's thought." Is Lindbeck correct in his assessment, or is it impossible to separate Luther from anti-Judaic and anti-Semitic rhetoric?

6. In what way can dogmas serve as aids in the reading of (the narratives of) Scripture?

7. Lindbeck argues that the church, as it becomes a minority, should not simply read the Sermon on the Mount apart from attention to the Tanakh or seek to live according to what society calls the "right side of history," but should seek ethical guidance by the Old Testament interpreted in the light of the New Testament. Given the lack of scriptural literacy within the church, is such an approach possible? Would it help the church maintain its identity in an increasingly secular society?

2

STUDENT

In this chapter, I will focus upon Lindbeck's student years, from the time he left China through the completion of his PhD program at Yale. In this chapter, I will focus upon some of Lindbeck's influential teachers, demonstrating how they prepared him for later work as an ecumenist and scholar of Roman Catholicism.

GUSTAVUS ADOLPHUS COLLEGE

Lindbeck left China in 1940 in order to attend Gustavus Adolphus College in St. Peter, Minnesota. Lindbeck felt like an alien when he arrived there. Everyone assumed he was an American because he spoke like one, but he had spent little time in America, and did not relate to the desires of his fellow students.[1]

In part due to his upbringing in China, Lindbeck did not assume that modernity was superior to other epochs,

1. Wright, "Israel," 116–17.

but instead just another time period with its own strengths and weaknesses. He also did not assume Western superiority. Because of this, he did not appreciate many of the modern authors that predominated in the curriculum during his education at Gustavus Adolphus, Yale, and Paris. Instead, he favored "an unlikely combination of, on the one hand, medieval thinkers and their contemporary interpreters such as [Jacques] Maritain [1882–1973] and [Étienne] Gilson [1884–1978], and, on the other hand, the Reformers and their neo-Orthodox successors (who were fashionable) and confessional Lutherans (who were not)."[2] Lindbeck majored in philosophy and was initially drawn to proofs for God's existence. As he went further in his studies, his interest in Catholic philosophy broadened to include theology, and so after graduating with his BA from Gustavus Adolphus in 1943, he went on to Yale Divinity School, where he received his BD (MDiv) in 1946. He then entered their PhD program.[3]

YALE

Discussing his education at Yale, Lindbeck mentions two of his professors as particularly influential: H. Richard Niebuhr (1894–1962) and Robert L. Calhoun (1896–1983). He says that they "taught me most about *how*—as distinct from *what*—to think theologically and historically."[4]

2. Lindbeck, "Confession and Community," 492–93.

3. Lindbeck, "Paris," 389, 92–93. Eckhart et al., "Guide to the George A. Lindbeck Papers" says that Lindbeck briefly studied at Augustana Theological Seminary in 1944, but this is the only reference I have seen about this.

4. Lindbeck, "Confession and Community," 496. He also discusses Paul Vignaux in this context, who will be discussed briefly later in this chapter.

H. Richard Niebuhr

H. Richard Niebuhr and his older brother Reinhold (1892–1971) were two of the most significant American theologians of the twentieth century. The Niebuhr brothers were the sons of Gustav Niebuhr, who was the pastor of a German Evangelical and Reformed Church in Wright City, Missouri. They both attended Elmhurst College, Eden Theological Seminary, and Yale, and also served as pastors. H. Richard received his BD from Yale in 1923 and PhD in 1924, writing a dissertation on Ernst Troeltsch (1865–1923). He briefly served as president of Elmhurst and professor of theology at Eden before returning to Yale as a professor in 1931. He taught there until his death in 1962. The brothers helped form a theological movement often called "Neo-Orthodoxy" that attempted to bring together the best of liberal Protestant theology and the classical Christian tradition by appropriating insights from Continental thinkers like Søren Kierkegaard and Karl Barth (1886–1968).[5]

In 1929, Niebuhr published *The Social Sources of Denominationalism*. Niebuhr begins the book saying, "Christianity has often achieved apparent success by ignoring the precepts of its founder."[6] Christians have drawn upon ambiguities within the Bible in order to justify their participation in various social evils, such as war or slavery. The church has, throughout its history, compromised. While the church cannot simply transcend the world in order to maintain purity, and while compromise is ultimately unavoidable, Niebuhr insists that the inevitability of compromise "does not make it less an evil."[7]

5. Livingston and Fiorenza, *Modern Christian Thought*, 165–68.
6. Niebuhr, *Social Sources*, 3.
7. Niebuhr, *Social Sources*, 5.

Niebuhr argues that the worst types of compromises are the unacknowledged ones, even when they are unconscious ones, for they are hypocritical and depart from "the faith that was once for all entrusted to the saints" (Jude 1:3). One such compromise is denominationalism, which involves not only denominational divisions between Christians—between Protestants and Catholics, Presbyterians and Methodists—but social divisions, such as national, racial, and economic divides. The gospel condemns denominationalism and divisiveness because Jesus opposed "class distinctions between the righteous few and the unhallowed many,"[8] and Paul said, "There is no longer Jew or Greek, there is no longer slave or free, there is no longer male and female; for all of you are one in Christ Jesus" (Gal 3:28). Despite this, and despite the fact that the church confesses faith in the "one, holy, catholic, and apostolic church," it has divided time and again through the centuries.

Many argue that these divisions resulted from doctrinal differences. They look at the different confessions of faith produced by the churches and compare and contrast their differences. These studies are not wholly inaccurate, but they are inadequate. There certainly were and are differences of opinion among and between the various Christian sects, but these were not simply differences of rationalization. Niebuhr argues instead that they were rooted "in more profound social divergences."[9] They stemmed from the various ways churches related to "national, economic, and cultural interests."[10] To explore this, Niebuhr engages the work of Troeltsch and Max Weber

8. Niebuhr, *Social Sources*, 7.
9. Niebuhr, *Social Sources*, 13.
10. Niebuhr, *Social Sources*, 18.

(1864–1920), who have "demonstrated how important are the differences in the sociological structure of religious groups in the determination of their doctrine."[11]

Lindbeck discusses the social role of division in the church in "Non-Theological Factors and Structures of Unity." In this 1998 essay, Lindbeck explores the relation of theological and non-theological factors in Christian unity and disunity. His reflections came out of his participation in *Facing Unity*, a report produced by the Joint Roman Catholic/Lutheran Commission in 1984. He notes that Christian unity in the first centuries of the church "was a matter of interdependence and mutual responsibility between otherwise autonomous local communities."[12] This stemmed initially from the personal relation between apostolic leaders, but as they died out, the church developed other means of maintaining communal interdependence. For example, bishops in neighboring areas participated in the consecration of each new bishop. This system, Lindbeck argues, was "flexible enough to accommodate theological differences as vast as those which separated Tertullian's Carthage from Origen's Alexandria, and yet it was also unified enough to produce a common scriptural canon together with liturgies and creeds which, despite regional variations, were harmonious rather than discordant."[13]

Non-theological factors both helped Christians maintain this unity and interdependence and played a role in early Christian divisions. He notes that their unity was maintained within Greek and Latin culture, whereas Punic-speaking Berbers gravitated toward Donatism while Syriac and Coptic speakers did not affirm Chalcedon.

---

11. Niebuhr, *Social Sources*, 17.

12. Lindbeck, "Non-Theological Factors," 134.

13. Lindbeck, "Non-Theological Factors," 134.

Various other non-theological factors influenced the church as it allied itself with the empire. Influential leaders like Charlemagne structured the church vertically, and this led to "the imperial papacy."[14] Such vertical unification has continued through the centuries in various forms—even within congregational and free church traditions—as well as within the ecumenical movement. He argues that with the rise of post-modernity's skepticism about previous structures of unity, new possibilities could arise for the ecumenical movement. He says in this context, "it makes sense to ask about the chances of a new pattern of ecumenical endeavor, one which builds from beneath rather than moves from above."[15]

New forms of unity may be possible because the contemporary context is more like the earliest centuries of the church than in any other intervening period. Christendom is largely passing away and the church is becoming a diaspora community. He notes, however, that there are still important differences between the contemporary context and the first centuries of the church, including diverse, elaborate organizational structures. Consequently, he argues, "the early church may provide precedents but not a blueprint for what we now need."[16] In order for the contemporary church to live as a single, particular people as it did in the early centuries, it must socialize its members in particular ecumenical forms of faithful Christian speech and practice, maintaining loyalty to the Lord Jesus Christ and mutual responsibility for one another.[17] In an endnote to the essay, Lindbeck credits Niebuhr, and in particular

14. Lindbeck, "Non-Theological Factors," 135.
15. Lindbeck, "Non-Theological Factors," 140.
16. Lindbeck, "Non-Theological Factors," 141.
17. Lindbeck, "Non-Theological Factors," 140–44.

Social Sources of Denominationalism, for mediating the work of Weber to him and influencing his thought.[18]

Robert L. Calhoun

More influential than Niebuhr was Lindbeck's doctoral supervisor, Robert Calhoun, a Congregationalist minister who taught at Yale from 1923 to 1965. Lindbeck remarks that "Calhoun's reputation was immense but ephemeral."[19] It stemmed more from his teaching than his publications. He taught not only in the divinity school and religion department, but also in the philosophy department. He was known for his year-long survey courses in the history of philosophy and the history of Christian doctrine. Lindbeck extolls him "as the greatest lecturer I have either heard or heard of. He was simultaneously both enthralling and intellectually demanding."[20] He had a breadth and depth of knowledge in a variety of subjects, but specialized in little, which is likely why he published very little. Lindbeck adds, however, that he and many of Calhoun's students have difficulty saying exactly how they are indebted to him.

Lindbeck claims that in many ways Calhoun remained a "liberal theologian" until his death, but he did so in such a way that he wound up being more doctrinally orthodox than "neo-orthodox" theologians like H. Richard Niebuhr,

---

18. Lindbeck, "Non-Theological Factors," 144n1. Lindbeck also credits his colleague, James Gustafson, and his book, *Treasures in Earthen Vessels* (Harper & Brothers, 1961). He further says, "My thinking on these matters has since been widened by, for example, Peter Berger, and Clifford Geertz, and through them, by Durkheim, but Weber's way of thinking, though not necessarily his conclusions, remain fundamental."

19. Lindbeck, "Introduction," x.

20. Lindbeck, "Introduction," xi.

for he combined a "methodological liberalism" with "doctrinal substance that was basically traditional."[21] He operated as a historical-critical historian within the classroom, and so it was difficult to pin him down confessionally:

> He acted in [such] a way [that] we didn't know—if you just listened to him when you were in his class—whether he was Protestant or Catholic. He always gave an understanding from the inside of each of the people he dealt with with historical finesse and knowledge. The result was that you got what felt like a sympathetic picture, because it was from the inside, explaining why Irenaeus thought the way he did; Tertullian, the way he did; Origen, the way he did.[22]

Calhoun taught students in such a way that even if they disagreed with the church's doctrinal developments, such as the christological and trinitarian dogmas, they at least made sense to them. This made it difficult for students to know exactly what Calhoun believed, but also made him acceptable to students from a diversity of backgrounds. He opened the door for liberal Protestants to mine the riches of the Christian tradition, thereby making possible a kind of *ressourcement*, "the return by divided Christians to the

---

21. Lindbeck, "Introduction," xviii. Lindbeck further discusses the relation of the traditional and liberal aspects throughout the introduction, but in particular on xxiv–xxxvi.

22. Wright, "Israel," 125. Lindbeck notes that Calhoun had the ability to do this not only in his course on the history of doctrine but philosophy as well. He notes, however, that neutrality was more highly respected in his time period than it is now (Lindbeck, "Introduction," xiv–xv). Lindbeck further discusses Calhoun's "methodological agnosticism" on xxxvi–xlvii. He concludes, "Calhoun's agnostic methods in philosophical and doctrinal history may have opened minds to matters before undreamt of, but this agnosticism was not by itself a heart-transforming force" (xlvii).

common sources of the faith."²³ He modeled the kind of "generous orthodoxy" that Lindbeck and his colleague and friend Hans Frei (1922–1988) touted in their work.²⁴ In using the historical method in ways that support rather than attack doctrinal development, Lindbeck claimed that Calhoun enabled him and many others to become ecumenists.²⁵ This was not accidental, for Calhoun himself noted the importance of the study of historical theology and the history of doctrine for ecumenism.²⁶ Calhoun also participated in the Federal and then National Council of Churches, as well as the World Council of Churches.²⁷ Lindbeck laments that by the time of Calhoun's death in 1983, Yale students began to lose enthusiasm for "doctrinally oriented ecumenism" or the kind of history of doctrine that Calhoun practiced.²⁸

Calhoun remained an influence upon Lindbeck's work throughout his life. The last piece of scholarship Lindbeck published was a revised version of Calhoun's lectures on the history of early Christian doctrine,²⁹ which includes an introduction by Lindbeck on Calhoun as a historical theologian.³⁰ Lindbeck began work on preparing

23. Lindbeck, "Introduction," xvi.

24. Lindbeck, "Introduction," xviiin10; xix–xxii.

25. Wright, "Israel," 126. See also Lindbeck, "Introduction," xvi–xvii.

26. See Calhoun, "The Role," 453–54.

27. Lindbeck, "Introduction," xii–xiii, lii.

28. Lindbeck, "Introduction," xvii.

29. Calhoun, *Scripture*.

30. Lindbeck, "Introduction," ix–lxx. Lindbeck's wife, Vi Lindbeck, and daughter, Kristen Lindbeck, as well as former student, Rebecca Frey, helped prepare the introduction for publication, working with different versions of the text that Lindbeck prepared (lxviiin97).

the manuscript in the 1980s, alongside Frei, but Frei's untimely death, as well as other factors, delayed completion of the project until 2011.[31]

Experience with Catholics at Yale

Lindbeck engaged more Roman Catholics at Yale. In fact, his best friend in Yale's philosophy department was a devout Catholic of whom he said, "I experienced the same sense of oneness in Christ that was familiar to me when growing up in China, except that with him it was unexpected."[32] It was because of him that the second article that Lindbeck published was about Roman Catholicism.[33] Lindbeck also served, for a time, as John Courtney Murray's (1904–1967) teaching assistant while Murray was a visiting professor in the philosophy department at Yale.[34] Due to the influence of some Franciscans he came to know, Lindbeck wrote his doctoral dissertation on the subtle doctor, John Duns Scotus (1266–1308).

TORONTO AND PARIS

While writing his dissertation at Yale, Lindbeck spent time in Toronto auditing classes at the Pontifical Institute for Medieval Studies under Étienne Gilson. Then he spent

---

31. Lindbeck, "Introduction," lxvi.

32. Lindbeck, "Paris," 393.

33. Lindbeck, "Catholicisme Américain." A few years later, Lindbeck also published, "Should the U.S.?"

34. Lindbeck, "Paris," 396. Lindbeck says that Murray, one of the most significant American Catholic thinkers of the time, was "the first Roman Catholic priest ever to teach at Yale in any capacity." For a brief analysis of Murray's life and work, see Lindbeck, "John Courtney Murray, S.J."

Student

almost two years, from 1949 to 1951, as a Fulbright Scholar in Paris at the École Pratique des Hautes Études, primarily under Paul Vignaux (1904–1987), a Roman Catholic layman who specialized in late medieval intellectual history.[35] He says of his study of medieval thought during this time, "It was as if my life were being designed in preparation for my later ecumenical work, even though I was oblivious to ecumenism."[36] He goes so far as to refer to his time in Paris as the beginning of his ecumenical journey.[37]

During this time, Lindbeck lacked interest in the ecumenism represented by groups like the Student Christian Movement, which he saw as "very much like the pan-Protestant interdenominationalism with which I was already familiar."[38] Despite his interest in Roman Catholic thought, he also did not appreciate the predominant Roman Catholic view of ecumenism of the time, which was an ecumenism of return—the view that other Christians must become Roman Catholic in order to bring about greater unity in the church.

In Paris, Lindbeck got to know some students from the Faculté de Théologie Protestante who were associated with the Reformed church. These students introduced Lindbeck to students from the Institute Catholique. Students from the two schools held meetings under the supervision of Jean Daniélou (1905–1974), a Jesuit theologian and later a cardinal who figured prominently among proponents

---

35. Wright, "I Pray," 58; Lindbeck, "Paris," 393; and Granfield, "George Lindbeck," 159.

36. Lindbeck, "Paris," 393.

37. Lindbeck, "Paris," 389.

38. Lindbeck, "Paris," 393.

of the *nouvelle théologie* (new theology).[39] Lindbeck says that "it became clear, as I came to know members of the French Catholic *avant-garde*, of whom Daniélou was one, that their goal was the visible unity of the churches, and that they thought this goal was attainable by methods other than simple return to Rome. My understanding of ecumenism and of Roman Catholic possibilities of change was revolutionized."[40]

These Catholics did not necessarily reject the language of "ecumenism of return," but they reinterpreted it. This point of view was typified by the French Dominican Yves Congar, whom Lindbeck considers to be "the greatest theologian of ecumenism that the Roman communion has yet seen."[41] Lindbeck says that Congar "had already argued in 1937, in the first major manifesto of Roman Catholic ecumenism, that 'return,' God-willing, will take place through profound and difficult reforms in Roman Catholicism and not only in the separated churches."[42] Lindbeck thus suggests that "convergence" is a better term than "return" for this future union of separated churches.

Though Congar argues that the so-called "Counter-Reformation," which he calls the "true reform of the Church,"[43] predates the Protestant Reformation, he still presents a sympathetic picture of Protestant Christians. In observing the spread of Protestant movements like

39. *Nouvelle théologie* refers to a twentieth-century school of Roman Catholic theology that sought to renew theology through *ressourcement*, a return to the sources (principally the writings of Thomas Aquinas). The principal figures were French theologians like Henri de Lubac, SJ (1896–1991) and Yves Congar, OP (1904–1995).

40. Lindbeck, "Paris," 394. See Wright, "I Pray," 58–59.

41. Lindbeck, "Paris," 394. See Wright, "I Pray," 60.

42. Lindbeck, "Paris," 394.

43. Congar, *Divided Christendom*, 19.

Lutheranism, he notes that if they have spread like they have throughout the globe, producing "remarkable lives consecrated to God," then "this must be due not to what they deny and reject, but to what they affirm and assert."[44] While perspectives like Congar's and Daniélou's later became commonplace, Lindbeck says that "they were astonishing in 1950 when I first encountered them."[45] For this reason, Protestants, like Karl Barth, were initially suspicious of these "naively hopeful Catholics."[46]

RETURN TO YALE

After his return to Yale, Lindbeck became an instructor in the philosophy department, teaching courses in medieval philosophy. He then received his PhD in 1955 and became an assistant professor.[47] He says that for a decade, he taught in both the philosophy department and the divinity school, but because he was primarily concerned with theology, he left the philosophy department.[48] He taught at Yale until his retirement in 1993.[49]

---

44. Congar, *Divided Christendom*, 39–40.

45. Lindbeck, "Paris," 394.

46. Lindbeck, "Paris," 395. Lindbeck says, "It was not until after Vatican II in the 1960s that Barth began admitting that the Roman Church could change in ways he had not anticipated."

47. Eckhart et al., "Guide to the George A. Lindbeck Papers."

48. Wright, "I Pray," 61.

49. Sterling, "George Lindbeck."

GEORGE LINDBECK

Discussion Questions

1. Lindbeck highlights two of his professors who greatly impacted his thought. What professors helped you become the person you are today?

2. H. Richard Niebuhr argues that while compromise is somewhat unavoidable, it is still an evil. Is this correct? If so, how should the church think about and respond to its past and current compromises?

3. Should the church accept denominationalism as normal or is it, as Niebuhr says, a compromise? Do we have another option, in our current context, besides denominationalism?

4. To what extent do nontheological factors play a role in church divisions?

5. Lindbeck discusses experiences that led to his interest in ecumenism. Have you had any experiences that have led you to embrace ecumenism?

3

MEDIEVALIST

MOST OF LINDBECK'S EARLY scholarship pertained to medieval philosophy and theology. As mentioned previously, he wrote his dissertation on the Franciscan John Duns Scotus, but he also published articles on Aristotle (384–322 BC), Abelard (1079–1142), and Pierre d'Ailly (1351–1420).[1] Above all, Lindbeck came under the influence of Thomas Aquinas (1225–1274). Though he once claimed that he was "probably not a Thomist,"[2] he later called himself a "Wittgensteinian Thomistic Lutheran."[3] He also said that the two theologians he engaged the most were Martin Luther and Thomas Aquinas.[4] Though Lindbeck published no articles specifically on medieval figures or topics after 1968, Bruce Marshall notes, "The exception is Thomas Aquinas, who has figured consistently in Lindbeck's writing and teaching

---

1. Lindbeck, "A Note"; Lindbeck, "Abelard"; Lindbeck, "Nominalism."

2. Lindbeck, "Thomism—Barrier or Bridge," 2A.

3. Lindbeck, "Review Essay," 235.

4. Lindbeck, *The Nature of Doctrine*, xxxi.

throughout his career and has deeply shaped his own theology, not least in *The Nature of Doctrine*.[5] This chapter will focus primarily on Lindbeck's earlier writing on Thomas, but will also seek to demonstrate that his training in medieval theology and philosophy impacted his work on Roman Catholicism and later participation in ecumenism.

THOMAS AQUINAS AS A BRIDGE OR BARRIER

While not every Catholic is a Thomist, the Roman Catholic Church has, in its official pronouncements, specifically held up Thomas's teachings. Pope Leo XIII referred to Thomas as "the chief and master of all towers."[6] Later, Pope Pius X held up scholastic philosophy, and in particular the philosophy of Thomas Aquinas, as "the basis of sacred studies."[7] And, of course, there are diverse interpretations of Thomas's thought. This makes it impossible to determine *the* Catholic view of Thomas, let alone *the* Protestant view. Lindbeck, however, does venture to offer his own view of Thomas—*a* Protestant view. He also sees Thomas "not as a representative of a particular party within western Christendom, but as one who belongs to us all," for Thomas "antedated the sixteenth century division of the Church, and he magisterially summed up the first twelve hundred years of the tradition."[8]

Lindbeck has a lofty view of Thomas. For example, he says, "Both Catholics and non-Catholics, among both

5. Marshall, "Introduction," xviii.
6. Leo XIII, *Aeterni Patris*, 17.
7. Pius X, *Doctoris Angelici*, para. 1.
8. Lindbeck, "Discovering Thomas (4)," 66. Cyril O'Regan says, "Mr. Lindbeck did not wax eloquent as to how much he loved Thomas Aquinas; he performed that love by teaching him as a master theologian for the entire Church" (O'Regan, "Quintessential," 25).

Medievalist

secular and religious historians of thought, agree that at least in the first fifteen hundred years of Christian history no man succeeded as well as Aquinas in developing a balanced and comprehensive view of the totality of reality. His great merit was combining scope of vision with systematic power and creative thought."[9] The superiority of Thomas's thought has garnered official sponsorship by the Roman Catholic Church even though he denies official dogmas, such as the Immaculate Conception of Mary.

Lindbeck argues that one can say this of Thomas whether or not one agrees with him, but as a Protestant, he wants to bring to Thomas's thought a particular question: "Is it true? Is it in conformity to the revelation witnessed in the Bible?"[10] To this question, Lindbeck gives a resounding yes. He argues that Thomism "is perhaps the most genuinely Christian of all fully elaborated philosophical theological world views."[11] In particular, from a Protestant perspective, he prefers it to any other school of Catholic thought, even for those who believe Thomas went too far in seeking to reconcile faith and reason, theology and philosophy.

Neither Luther nor Calvin offered such a system, and later Protestants who did offer such systems, like Anglican Richard Hooker (1554–1600),[12] were influenced by Thomas. After Jonathan Edwards (1703–1758), one must wait until the nineteenth and twentieth centuries to see post-Kantian systems developed by theologians like Friedrich Schleiermacher (1768–1834) and Paul

9. Lindbeck, "Thomism—Barrier or Bridge," 2A. See Lindbeck, "Thomism," 361.

10. Lindbeck, "Thomism—Barrier or Bridge," 2A.

11. Lindbeck, "Thomism—Barrier or Bridge," 2A.

12. The text of this article, "Thomism—Barrier or Bridge," actually says Thomas Hooker, but this appears to be a misprint.

Tillich (1886–1965). Even a Protestant thinker like Karl Barth (1886–1968), who despises Thomas's *analogia entis* ("analogy of being"), prefers Thomas to these latter Protestants. Lindbeck thus concludes, "Aquinas is much more faithful to the Christian Gospel than have been most other Christian systematic thinkers."[13]

Lindbeck considers the possibility that if Thomas was more well-known at the time of the Reformation, that the schism between Catholics and Protestants may have been avoided. While Reformers like Luther are critical of Thomas, Lindbeck contends that Luther only knew the corrupt Thomists of his own time, and not Thomas's own works.[14] Lindbeck claims, "[Thomas] was certainly closer to the Reformation than were the Catholic theologians they spent their time fighting."[15]

Lindbeck points out that Thomas affirmed that we are saved by grace alone (*sola gratia*), and he did so more strongly than Catholics in the sixteenth century. Thomas rejected Pelagianism and semi-Pelagianism, and he affirmed the Augustinian view that God alone saves—a view that is shared by Luther and Calvin.[16] Elsewhere, Lindbeck points to the overlap between Thomas's discussion of hope and Luther's discussion of faith. First, Thomas emphasizes that Christian hope is "in God's goodness *pro nobis* ['for us']."[17] He clarifies that hope "makes us adhere to God, as the source whence we derive perfect goodness, i.e., insofar as, by hope, we trust to the Divine assistance for

---

13. Lindbeck, "Thomism—Barrier or Bridge," 2A.

14. Lindbeck, "Thomism—Barrier or Bridge," 2A; Lindbeck, "Discovering Thomas (4)," 70.

15. Lindbeck, "Thomism—Barrier or Bridge," 2A.

16. Lindbeck, "Thomism—Barrier or Bridge," 2A.

17. Lindbeck, "Discovering Thomas (4)," 68.

obtaining happiness."[18] Lindbeck thus argues that just as we can speak of Luther's "fiducial faith," passages like this demonstrate that we can likewise speak of Thomas's "fiducial hope."[19] Second, Thomas recognizes that "the ultimate basis for this fiducial hope is God alone,"[20] for hope "does not derive from our merits, but from grace alone."[21] Third, though many have assumed that Thomas would have opposed Luther's *Heilsgewissheit* ("assurance of salvation"), Lindbeck argues that this is not the case. Thomas argues in his discussion of hope that "whoever has faith is certain of God's omnipotence and mercy."[22]

This does not mean there are no obvious differences between Thomas and Luther. Thomas certainly differs from the Reformers in his understanding of first and second causes. He gives God the glory for all that God does without denying human freedom or making humanity passive.[23] He also speaks of the "freedom of the will" and of "meriting salvation," albeit while arguing that this freedom to cooperate with God is "rigorously and totally the gift of grace."[24] Though Thomas does not speak of justification by faith alone (*sola fide*) as the Reformers do, Lindbeck argues that this differences "is more terminological than real."[25]

Scripture is another area where Lindbeck contends Thomas is closer to the Reformers than post-Tridentine

18. Aquinas, *Summa Theologiae*, II–II.17.6.
19. Lindbeck, "Discovering Thomas (4)," 68.
20. Lindbeck, "Discovering Thomas (4)," 68.
21. Aquinas, *Summa Theologiae*, II–II.17.1.ad 2.
22. Aquinas, *Summa Theologiae*, II–II.18.4.ad 2.
23. Lindbeck, "Thomism—Barrier or Bridge," 2A–3A.
24. Lindbeck, "Discovering Thomas (4)," 69.
25. Lindbeck, "Discovering Thomas (4)," 69.

thinkers. For Thomas, the primary work of the theologian is the interpretation of Scripture. This, of course, does not mean he denied the importance of the doctors, councils, and confessions of the church. Rather, he understood these as "guides to the interpretation of Scripture rather than as sources of theology."[26] This does not make Thomas a Protestant, but neither does it make him a post-Tridentine Catholic.[27]

While Augustine is generally assumed to be closer to the Reformers than Thomas due to Augustine's influence upon the Reformers, Lindbeck identifies two further areas in which the Reformers are closer to Thomas. First, Thomas advocated for the independence of the sciences. "He insisted that reason in its sphere must do its own work in its own way and so he utterly rejected that mixing of faith and reason which was so characteristic of the Augustinian tradition."[28] Lindbeck argues that the Protestant tradition has largely followed Thomas here.

Second, drawing upon Aristotle, Thomas argued that the soul is the form of the body, and thus rejected the dualism of body and soul that Augustine and others adopted from Plato. While some in Thomas's day were concerned this would lead to the rejection of the immortality of the soul, Lindbeck argues that this view brought Thomas closer to a biblical anthropology. So, while even Protestants have been influenced by Augustinian dualism, Lindbeck argues that they should embrace the unity of the human.[29]

---

26. Lindbeck, "Thomism—Barrier or Bridge," 3A.
27. Lindbeck, "Thomism—Barrier or Bridge," 3A.
28. Lindbeck, "Thomism—Barrier or Bridge," 3A.
29. Lindbeck, "Thomism—Barrier or Bridge," 3A.

Medievalist

As Lindbeck says, "Man is a soul-body unity, not a soul using a body."[30]

Some contemporary Protestant theologians may reject these bridges between Thomas and the Reformation tradition as superficial, and may thus see Thomism as a barrier between Catholics and Protestants. For them, Thomas places too great of an emphasis upon natural reason in his arguments for God's existence. Lindbeck defends Thomas on this point, however, noting that his famous five ways are not proofs in the same sense as a geometric proof. They do not deny the need for grace. Instead, "The kind of rationality which they make use of is of a higher sort which demands that a man be open to existence to its wonder, its radical and frightening contingency, and its depth."[31] One does not argue oneself into faith, but instead comes to worship the Almighty God revealed in creation. Thus, there is less of a conflict between Thomas and the reformers on the relation of faith and reason, of philosophy and theology, than is generally assumed.[32]

Lindbeck does, however, affirm one aspect of this Protestant objection to Thomas—that Thomas discusses grace in impersonal terms, rather than dynamic and personal ones. He asks, "Isn't the whole notion of grace as infused, created habitus radically un-Christian, and isn't Aquinas committed to such a view just because he has utilized philosophical, Aristotelian categories in developing this theology?"[33] While Thomas affirms that God

---

30. Lindbeck, "Discovering Thomas (3)," 72. See Lindbeck, "Thomism," 361–62.

31. Lindbeck, "Thomism—Barrier or Bridge," 3A.

32. Lindbeck, "Discovering Thomas (1)," 47.

33. Lindbeck, "Thomism—Barrier or Bridge," 3A.

alone is responsible for salvation, does his understanding of grace and of the sacraments undermine this view? So, while Lindbeck points to ways in which Thomas may be a bridge instead of a barrier, he ultimately leaves this question unanswered.

THOMAS AND CLASSICAL CHRISTIAN THEISM

In commenting on the early questions of the Prima Pars ("first part") of the *Summa Theologiae*, those often associated with the *de deo uno* ("on the oneness of God"), Lindbeck questions the popular notion that they constitute a "natural theology" as opposed to the "revealed theology" of the *de deo trino* ("on the Trinity"). He contends, "St. Thomas knows only the single science of *sacra doctrina*, and he does not divide it into revealed and unrevealed parts."[34] Thomas uses philosophical arguments to discuss the oneness of God and the Trinity, just as he draws upon Scripture in both. As Thomas famously argues,

> Since therefore grace does not destroy nature but perfects it, natural reason should minister to faith as the natural bent of the will ministers to charity. Hence the Apostle says: *Bringing into captivity every understanding unto the obedience of Christ* (2 Cor 10:5). Hence sacred doctrine makes use also of the authority of philosophers in those questions in which they were able to know the truth by natural reason, as Paul quotes a saying of Aratus: *As some also of your own poets said: For we are also His offspring* (Acts 17:28). Nevertheless, sacred doctrine makes use of these authorities as extrinsic and probable arguments, but properly uses the authority of

---

34. Lindbeck, "Discovering Thomas (1)," 46.

> the canonical Scriptures as an incontrovertible proof, and the authority of the doctors of the Church as one that may properly be used, yet merely as probable. For our faith rests upon the revelation made to the apostles and prophets who wrote the canonical books, and not on the revelations (if any such there are) made to other doctors.[35]

For example, the famous "five ways"[36] are not proofs in the strict sense, but probabilistic arguments that demonstrate, in Paul's words, that "[God's] eternal power and divine nature, invisible though they are, have been understood and seen through the things he has made" (Rom 1:20).[37]

Lindbeck views Thomas's discussion of *de deo uno* as "the classic systematic presentation of traditional Christian theism."[38] In it, Thomas gathers together the collected wisdom of the church, both East and West, on God's being and perfection: that God is simple, perfect, good, infinite, immutable and impassible, eternal, one, omnipotent and omniscient, true, love, just, and first and foremost, *ipsum esse*—Being Itself. Lindbeck argues, "No conceptual construct has more successfully symbolized God's unsurpassable majesty."[39] Lindbeck notes that despite this, some no longer think that Thomas's view of God is viable. They question whether it coheres with the picture of the living God provided in Scripture.

He argues, however, that one does not need to understand Thomas this way. There are two reasons for this.

---

35. Aquinas, *Summa Theologiae*, I.8.ad 2.

36. Aquinas, *Summa Theologiae*, I.2.

37. Lindbeck, "Discovering Thomas (1)," 47; Lindbeck, *The Nature of Doctrine*, 117.

38. Lindbeck, "Discovering Thomas (1)," 48.

39. Lindbeck, "Discovering Thomas (1)," 48.

First, Lindbeck draws upon the work of French Dominican A. G. Sertillanges (1863–1948), who argues that Thomas is not discussing realities found in God, but the names of God.⁴⁰ As Thomas says, "[I]n this life we cannot see the essence of God; but we know God from creatures as their principle, and also by way of excellence and remotion. In this way therefore He can be named by us from creatures, yet not so that the name which signifies Him expresses the divine essence in itself."⁴¹ Lindbeck says, "For centuries this has been over-looked despite the fact that Aquinas insists that he is talking on the linguistic, not the ontological level."⁴² We also see other Wittgensteinian Thomists, like Victor Preller (1931–2001), David Burrell (1933–), and Herbert McCabe (1926–2001) holding to similar views.⁴³

Second, Lindbeck says, "Aquinas is equally insistent that his theory of analogical predication means that although what the divine names signify is truly found in God, their mode of signification is entirely different from any with which we are acquainted."⁴⁴ By this Lindbeck means that while we know that a certain name is properly said of God, like "God is good," the use of the term "good"

---

40. Lindbeck, "Discovering Thomas (1)," 49. Sertillanges refers to this as Thomas's "agnosticism." See Lindbeck, *The Nature of Doctrine*, 53 and 53n28.

41. Aquinas, *Summa Theologiae*, I.13.1c.

42. Lindbeck, "Discovering Thomas (1)," 49.

43. See Preller, *Divine Science*; Burrell, *Aquinas*, 5–87; McCabe, *God Matters*, 5–11, 40–41; and Manni, *Herbert McCabe*, 81–98. Lindbeck expresses indebtedness to Preller, Burrell, and the "philosophical/analytic" approach to Thomas in Wright, "I Pray," 68–70. See also Wright, "The Silent Shifting," 43–52.

44. Lindbeck, "Discovering Thomas (1)," 49. See Lindbeck, *The Nature of Doctrine*, 52, where Lindbeck distinguishes between the *modus significandi*, the human mode of signifying, and the *significatum*.

there is so radically different from when it is used to describe a dog, a person, or a piece of pizza that we do not properly know the meaning of "good" when it is applied to God. We will have to wait until we see God face to face before we can understand these terms, and then, we will no longer need them.[45]

If Thomas does not provide us with information about God, then why does he take the time to write this treatise? Lindbeck contends, "They do not describe God, they do not tell us who he is, but rather indicate the context within which scriptural and creedal descriptions of who God is (e.g., the Trinity, the Father of Jesus Christ, etc.) can be given a specific referent."[46] God is the explanation of all that exists. In God, "essence and existence are identical," and all the attributes of God flow from this assertion.[47]

Lindbeck notes another reason why Thomas takes the time to discuss how we should properly speak of God, even though we do not always know what the words mean. Various philosophers have noted that language is not only used to convey information. For example, Wittgenstein argues that humans use a variety of "language games" in order to speak. These demonstrate that speaking a language is an activity or a "form of life." Wittgenstein points to a number of possible language games:

> Giving orders, and acting on them—
> Describing an object by its appearance, or by its measurements—
> Constructing an object from a description (a drawing)—
> Reporting an event—

45. Lindbeck, "Discovering Thomas (1)," 49; Lindbeck, *The Nature of Doctrine*, 52–53.

46. Lindbeck, "Discovering Thomas (1)," 50.

47. Lindbeck, "Discovering Thomas (1)," 50.

Speculating about the event—
Forming and testing a hypothesis—
Presenting the results of an experiment in tables and diagrams—
Making up a story; and reading one—
Acting in a play—
Singing rounds—
Guessing riddles—
Cracking a joke; telling one—
Solving a problem in applied arithmetic—
Translating from one language to another—
Requesting, thanking, cursing, greeting, praying.[48]

Building upon Wittgenstein's view of language, Lindbeck says,

> [Language] is the vehicle of prayer and praise, worship and doxology, to mention simply some of its "religious" functions. In all these activities God is named, and thereby feelings are elicited and passions, attitudes and actions molded and directed. This is what makes it important that we use the right names. Those who learn to speak of God rightly may not know what they are saying in any cognitively significant sense, but yet their very beings may be transformed into conformity with him who alone is the high and mighty one. This is why scripture gives certain names to God even while insisting that he is essentially unnameable, and this is why theologians such as Aquinas spend so much time relating the biblical names to other ways (e.g., Aristotelian ways) of speaking about God even while recognizing that no specifiable information is communicated thereby.[49]

---

48. Wittgenstein, *Philosophical Investigations*, §23.
49. Lindbeck, "Discovering Thomas (1)," 51. See also Lindbeck,

Lindbeck acknowledges all of this while showing less confidence that the language of thirteenth-century Aristotelian thought remains relevant in the twentieth century.

Lindbeck argues that the reason why so many have misunderstood Thomas is that they have ignored the first pages of the *Summa Theologiae*. In the first article of the first question, Thomas argues that Scripture was not discovered by human reason but was inspired by God. Because of this, he says, "there should be another science inspired by God."[50] And Thomas makes it clear that this God is the God and Father of Jesus Christ. Thomas continues, in the *Secunda Secundae*, "Unbelievers cannot be said *to believe in a God* as we understand it in relation to the act of faith. For they do not believe that God exists under the conditions that faith determines; hence they do not truly believe in a God, since, as the Philosopher observes (*Metaph*. ix, text. 22) to know simple things defectively is not to know them at all."[51] Lindbeck says of this, "It is thus no exaggeration to say that, for St. Thomas, those who believe only in the existence of the God of *De Deo Uno* fall as far short of believing that there is a God as the man who simply asserts that there sometime existed a being at approximately 38 degrees north and 24 degrees east falls short of believing that Socrates once lived."[52]

THOMAS AND THE TRINITY

Lindbeck notes that Protestants like Karl Barth and Catholics like Karl Rahner (1904–1984) fault Thomas

---

The Nature of Doctrine, 53.

50. Aquinas, *Summa Theologiae*, I.1.1.c.

51. Aquinas, *Summa Theologiae*, II-II.2.2.ad 3.

52. Lindbeck, "Discovering Thomas (1)," 52.

and the Western Christian tradition for not starting their trinitarian reflection with the economic Trinity. Lindbeck faults these critics for not reading Thomas in his historical context. When one does so, "there is no more need to be scandalized by the Aristotelian complexities of his trinitarian speculation than at the Melchizedekian features of the Christology of Hebrews."[53]

Lindbeck begins setting Thomas within his context by highlighting an area in which Barth and Rahner agree with Thomas, namely, that there is an immanent Trinity. Apart from this understanding, God is not the triune God—Father, Son, and Spirit—who revealed Godself. Lindbeck says, "In short, the whole of faith, all that is distinctively Christian about the fullness and finality of God's self-giving in Jesus Christ and through the Holy Spirit, involves asserting that the economic is also the immanent Trinity."[54] So within the *Summa Theologiae*, he asserts, Thomas could have started with the economic Trinity, with God's work in creation, incarnation, and redemption. Thomas himself demonstrated an openness to alternative trinitarian formulations in the *Summa Contra Gentiles* (4, cc. 2–26) and *De Potentia* (qq. 2, 8–10).

Despite this, modern readers still critique Thomas's treatment of the immanent Trinity. Lindbeck says that they often see it as "tedious" and "more than useless," or even as "a manifestation of *hubris*."[55] Lindbeck counters that this too ignores the historical context in which Thomas taught and wrote. He did not invent the questions that he raised; they were debated topics within his day. Thomas did not, Lindbeck argues, "have an exaggerated estimate of

53. Lindbeck, "Discovering Thomas (2)," 46.
54. Lindbeck, "Discovering Thomas (2)," 46.
55. Lindbeck, "Discovering Thomas (2)," 47.

what he was doing."[56] Though he appropriates Augustine's psychological analogy of the Trinity, Thomas acknowledges that "some other theory might explain them."[57] Lindbeck argues that Thomas could very well have recognized the legitimacy of a different trinitarian understanding, such as the one proposed by the Cappadocians or by various modern thinkers.

He then calls upon contemporary theologians to be as gracious as Thomas is and to recognize the strengths of his approach. For example, Thomas is certainly right not to identify each of the persons of the Trinity with a certain attribute, "for then God would be thought of in subordinationist or modalistic fashion as subject and beyond the Persons."[58] Second, Thomas is correct in not seeing each of the persons as a "center of consciousness" as social trinitarians do, for this, Lindbeck argues, is "quite simply, tritheistic."[59] Third, Lindbeck argues that it is not clear that anyone has made any advances on the traditional proposals. It is preferable to follow the traditional understanding that the persons are "processional 'relations' within the divine unity"—and to utilize the psychological analogy of the Son and Spirit as "reflexive relations of self-knowledge and love."[60] Still Lindbeck concludes that "it is not the immanent, but economic Trinity which is the center of Christian thought and life."[61] As a Lutheran, Lindbeck follows Philip Melanchthon's dictum that "to know God is to

---

56. Lindbeck, "Discovering Thomas (2)," 47.
57. Aquinas, *Summa Theologiae*, I.32.1.ad 2.
58. Lindbeck, "Discovering Thomas (2)," 48.
59. Lindbeck, "Discovering Thomas (2)," 48.
60. Lindbeck, "Discovering Thomas (2)," 48.
61. Lindbeck, "Discovering Thomas (2)," 48.

know his benefits."⁶² He then contends, "It is the evidence of the genius of Aquinas that he in principle recognizes this even though, in practice, he was a child of his times and discussed the Trinity almost exclusively from a secondary perspective."⁶³

CONCLUSION: MEDIEVAL THOUGHT AS PREPARATION FOR STUDY OF CONTEMPORARY ROMAN CATHOLICISM AND ECUMENICAL DIALOGUE

It is undeniably true that Lindbeck's invitation to serve as an observer at Vatican II changed the trajectory of his career. As Bruce Marshall says, "Lindbeck might have remained primarily a historian of medieval thought had it not been for the Second Vatican Council."⁶⁴ Despite the changes in emphasis in his published work, one can see that his work as a medievalist prepared him for his later work. Lindbeck argues that was the point. He did not necessarily have a passion for medieval philosophy and theology. He came to observe that "Catholics were doing a lot more good scholarly work on Protestants, particularly Karl Barth, than any Protestants were doing about contemporary Catholic developments."⁶⁵ And, especially at that time, the way to become an expert in contemporary Roman Catholicism was through study of the Middle Ages.

One could also argue that Lindbeck's study of medieval philosophy and theology helped prepare him for his later ecumenical work. He actually makes the comparison

62. Lindbeck, "Discovering Thomas (2)," 48.
63. Lindbeck, "Discovering Thomas (2)," 48.
64. Marshall, "Introduction," ix.
65. Wright, "I Pray," 57–58.

between the medieval approach of raising questions, as seen in Thomas, and ecumenical dialogue. He says,

> You raise a question, and then there is an objection to the position that you're going to take, and then you try to answer the objection. I would say that what I'm trying to do in *The Nature of Doctrine*—[to develop] a so-called rule theory of doctrine, a grammatical rule theory of doctrine—is an attempt then to provide a supporting conceptuality for seeing how this "question method" proceeds and how apparently contradictory views can be shown not to contradict each other [if one illustrates] the appropriate distinctions.[66]

After discussing Lindbeck's time as an observer at Vatican II, I will return to a discussion of his understanding of ecumenical dialogue.

Discussion Questions

1. Can Thomas Aquinas be seen as a bridge figure between Catholics and Protestants? If so/not, why?
2. Lindbeck argues that both Thomas and Luther affirm that we are saved by grace alone and that there is overlap between Thomas's understanding of hope and Luther's view of faith. Does he make a convincing case?
3. Is the primary work of theology the interpretation of Scripture?
4. How does the classical picture of God relate to the one provided in Scripture?

---

66. Wright, "I Pray," 72.

5. What does it mean to speak of God analogically?
6. Is Lindbeck correct that the economic Trinity is "the center of Christian thought and life"?

4

OBSERVER

In 1959, Lindbeck received a Morse Fellowship from Yale University to study in Tübingen, Germany. While he was in Germany, Pope John XXIII called for the Second Vatican Council. Bishop Kristen Skydsgaard (1902–1990), working for the Lutheran World Federation, brought together a group of Lutherans to discuss how they should prepare for the council. Skydsgaard invited Lindbeck to participate. Out of this meeting, it was decided that a book should be written, entitled *The Papal Council and the Gospel: Protestant Theologians Evaluate the Coming Vatican Council* (Augsburg, 1961), which was edited by Skydsgaard and simultaneously published in both English and German.[1] Lindbeck penned an article in the volume entitled, "Roman Catholicism on the Eve of the Council."

Within the essay, Lindbeck argues that from a Protestant perspective, contemporary Roman Catholicism consists of two contrasting tendencies. First, there is an

1. Wright, "I Pray," 61–62.

increased focus upon "central Christian realities," which Lindbeck describes as a "genuine 'evangelical revival' within the Roman Church."[2] This can be seen in the progress in Catholic study of the Bible by both scholars and general readers, a re-evaluation of the Protestant Reformation and the language used of Protestants, the elimination of clerical abuses of power, liturgical reform, recognition of the universal priesthood of all Christians, and renewed emphasis upon God's saving work in Christ.[3] Second, there are movements that are contrary to this evangelical revival, such as the increased emphasis upon Marian dogmas like the Immaculate Conception and the Assumption.[4] While Protestants may be perplexed about how both of these tendencies can develop alongside each other, one cannot ignore either tendency to get a well-rounded picture of the Catholic landscape.[5]

Lindbeck argues that it is likely out of his participation in this discussion group and volume that he was invited to be an observer at the Second Vatican Council, though there were also other factors.[6] Pope John XXIII

2. Lindbeck, "Roman Catholicism," 61.

3. Lindbeck, "Roman Catholicism," 68–78. Lindbeck also points to the "increase in historical study and consciousness" as seen in Yves Congar and others associated with *resourcement* (85–86).

4. Lindbeck, "Roman Catholicism," 61. See 79–81, where Lindbeck seeks to "indicate in an extremely general way the character of what might be called evangelical Roman Catholic Mariology" (80) as opposed to the "Mariolatry" present within the Roman Catholic Church.

5. Lindbeck says, "Roman Catholicism varies enormously from one part of the world to another," and goes on to note that the first tendency is more common in French and German speaking areas of Europe, as well as the Low Countries, while the second prevails in Spain, Italy, and Latin America (62).

6. Wright, "I Pray," 62. He believes that Skydsgaard convinced

invited various world confessional organizations, such as the Lutheran World Federation (LWF), to delegate three observers to the council. At the time of the Council, the United States was a major source of funding, and so the LWF decided one of their three observers must be an American. They also wanted someone who knew Latin, German, and French, had exposure to Roman Catholic theology, and would be able to obtain a leave of absence from their job. Lindbeck says, "They scraped the bottom of the barrel, and at the bottom there was an untenured Yale teacher whose dean and department were not bound by the draconian faculty employment rules now in effect."[7]

At the opening of the first session of Vatican II, there were forty-some Delegated Observers. This number grew to over ninety at the last session. The LWF also initially sent Skydsgaard and Hungarian scholar Vilmos Vajta (1918–1998), but later also sent American Warren Quanbeck (1917–1979) and German Edmund Schlink. Others were also appointed for shorter periods of time. Lindbeck clarifies, "My role, as befitted my junior status, was to take up residence in Rome together with my family in order to provide what information I could about what was happening between sessions."[8] Lindbeck, his wife Violet (1927–2021, m. 1953), and young daughter, Kristen (b. 1960),[9] resided in Rome between 1962 and 1964. Between sessions, he maintained contacts in Rome and traveled on

---

Franklin Clark Frye (1900–1968), an important figure in the Lutheran Church in America at the time, to send Lindbeck.

7. Weigel, "Re-Viewing Vatican II," 44.

8. Lindbeck, "Paris," 399. Lindbeck says, "As far as I know, only one other Delegated Observer, the Anglican canon Bernard Pawley (who was also accompanied by his family), was resident in Rome for the intersessions" (399n22).

9. Thanks to Kris Lindbeck for providing these dates.

behalf of the LWF, informing Lutherans of the progress of the council and attending events like the Montreal meeting of Faith and Order in 1963.[10] Lindbeck contributed numerous articles to various journals and magazines and contributed to two further volumes with Skysdgaard and company, editing one of them.[11]

THE FUTURE OF ROMAN CATHOLIC THEOLOGY

In August 1966, Lindbeck gave a series of lectures on Vatican II and the future of Roman Catholicism at Concordia Seminary in St. Louis. These lectures later became *The Future of Roman Catholic Theology*.[12] In the volume, Lindbeck weighs in on the various themes present within the Council's documents, seeking to identify their unique contributions to theology.[13] He does so with the knowledge that the documents are in a sense "ambiguous, open to both rigidly 'conservative' and radically 'progressive' exegesis,"[14] as the last half century of interpretation has demonstrated. Lindbeck contends that the way one reads the documents depends upon how one understands their place within and influence upon theological developments within the Roman Catholic Church and within other churches. He sees Vatican II as a "transitional phase" between what came before and what will come after, bringing together the old and the new. This means that one cannot simply restate what the Council's documents say. He says, "My own

10. Weigel, "Re-Viewing Vatican II, 44.

11. Lindbeck edited *Dialogue* and Quanbeck edited *Challenge*.

12. I decided for the purposes of this volume to focus primarily on *The Future of Roman Catholic Theology* because it synthesizes much of his previous writing on Vatican II.

13. Lindbeck, *The Future of Roman Catholic Theology*, 2.

14. Lindbeck, *The Future of Roman Catholic Theology*, 3.

view . . . is that because the Council is part of a dynamic, ongoing process, it is the *new* theological emphases which are likely to prove most significant as a basis and guide for further developments. As a matter of fact, the majority of the most active drafters and interpreters of the documents understand them as favoring fresh approaches."[15] So while not ignoring "the old" within the council documents, Lindbeck emphasizes "the patterns of thought which make Vatican II theologically distinctive and radically different from the two previous councils and the last four hundred years of Roman Catholic dogmatic development."[16]

In order to achieve this, Lindbeck focuses in chapter 1 on how the Council discusses the "world" and in chapters 2 through 5 on "church and mission." He explains that "'Church and mission' is handled as a single topic because, according to one strong strain of thought at the Council, 'church *is* mission.'"[17] He divides this emphasis upon church and mission into four different facets: *diakonia*, or service to the world; *leitourgia*, or worship; *koinonia*, or communal unity; and common faith or dogma. He says, "This pattern of exposition reflects the inner logic, though not always the external divisions, of the Council's sixteen documents."[18] Within this approach, he sees *Lumen Gentium*, the Dogmatic Constitution of the Church, as "the centerpiece of the Council," which is "complemented by the Constitution on the Church in the Modern World [*Gaudium et Spes*]."[19] The various other documents also address these themes in various ways.

15. Lindbeck, *The Future of Roman Catholic Theology*, 4.
16. Lindbeck, *The Future of Roman Catholic Theology*, 4.
17. Lindbeck, *The Future of Roman Catholic Theology*, 5.
18. Lindbeck, *The Future of Roman Catholic Theology*, 5.
19. Lindbeck, *The Future of Roman Catholic Theology*, 5.

World

Lindbeck argues that in order to grasp what the Council says about the church and its mission, one must first seek to understand its "new vision" of the world: "This new vision grows out of a new understanding of biblical eschatology together with the acceptance of a secular-scientific world view."[20] They came to replace a classical "two-storied" or "three-storied" view of the universe, one with a lower level of time and matter and an upper, immaterial level which consists of angels and God, with a "realistically futuristic" eschatology.[21] Though Lindbeck acknowledges the benefits and contributions of various versions of the classical picture—which developed in dialogue with Greek thought—he argues that it ultimately falls short of the biblical picture, for the divide in Scripture is not between the material and immaterial, but between the old age and the new age that has begun in Christ and will come to fulfillment with the restoration and redemption of the cosmos.[22] This "new" view shifts the focus from an individualistic understanding of judgment and salvation to a communal and cosmic view of redemption, which moves the general resurrection from an "addendum to theological treatises" to "the vivid focus of hope for the world's salvation."[23] Lindbeck argues that contemporary scholars, both Protestants and Catholics, have been drawn to biblical eschatology not only to be faithful to the biblical witness and salvation history, but because "the eschatology of the New Testament makes sense in the modern framework in a way that it could not

20. Lindbeck, *The Future of Roman Catholic Theology*, 9.

21. Lindbeck, *The Future of Roman Catholic Theology*, 9, 12.

22. Lindbeck, *The Future of Roman Catholic Theology*, 12–15, 23. See *Lumen Gentium*, §48.

23. Lindbeck, *The Future of Roman Catholic Theology*, 14.

in the classical outlook."[24] They have moved, as *Gaudium et Spes* says, "from a rather static concept of reality to a more dynamic, evolutionary one."[25]

Church and Mission

Accompanying this new conception of the world is a "new vision of the church"—one shared, in various ways, by both Protestants and Catholics. It sees the church as "the messianic pilgrim people of God, the sacramental sign (or, as a Protestant might be more inclined to say, 'witness') to the kingdom which has begun and will be consummated in Christ."[26] So first, the church is a pilgrim people, one that has not yet reached its goal. Second, the church is mission and it has a mission that "differentiates this people from other peoples."[27] Rather than identifying the church and the kingdom, as some in the classical perspective like Pseudo-Dionysius or Robert Bellarmine had, this perspective argues that the church "points and strives towards the kingdom."[28] The view of the church as a pilgrim people and sacramental sign depends in various ways upon biblical and patristic sources—sources that are older than the "classic" or "traditional" views of the church.

---

24. Lindbeck, *The Future of Roman Catholic Theology*, 17. Lindbeck argues, "It can even be made to appear as an historicized and eschatological version of certain emphases of St. Thomas Aquinas (e.g., that grace does not destroy but perfects nature, or that the soul is the form of the body). Nevertheless, it is fundamentally different from the sixteenth-century scholasticisms to which the Reformers objected" (20).

25. *Gaudium et Spes*, §5.

26. Lindbeck, *The Future of Roman Catholic Theology*, 27.

27. Lindbeck, *The Future of Roman Catholic Theology*, 27.

28. Lindbeck, *The Future of Roman Catholic Theology*, 29.

The Council documents do not consistently display these newer views of the church, but rather they bring together both newer and older views. While *Lumen Gentium* brings together "three views of the church—as sacrament, pilgrim people, and institution of salvation," and they are "juxtaposed without any clear indication of their systematic priorities or interrelationships,"[29] there is a sense in which *Lumen Gentium* seeks to avoid three particular ecclesiological vices: "juridical institutionalism, clericalism, and triumphalism."[30] *Lumen Gentium* begins by discussing the church as a mystery, but in doing so, it "uses *heilsgeschichtliche* [salvation history] rather than nature-supernature categories."[31] It describes the church as "a sacrament—a sign and instrument, that is, of communion with God and of the unity of the entire human race."[32] This chapter includes the infamous phrase that the Roman Catholic Church is not identical with "the church," but rather the church "subsists in the Catholic Church." It also claims that "many elements of sanctification and truth are found outside of its visible confines."[33]

Lumen Gentium then moves on in chapter 2 to discuss the church as the pilgrim people of God. The chapter begins by saying, "[God] has . . . willed to make women

---

29. Lindbeck, *The Future of Roman Catholic Theology*, 32. It is in chapter 3 that *Lumen Gentium* discusses the hierarchy of the church, including the pope and the bishops. Within this chapter, Lindbeck argues, "we encounter the non-eschatological, non-historical categories of the classical outlook" (32).

30. Lindbeck, *The Future of Roman Catholic Theology*, 30. Lindbeck also acknowledges that while Protestants have often denounced these vices, they have also been guilty of them (35).

31. Lindbeck, *The Future of Roman Catholic Theology*, 32.

32. *Lumen Gentium*," §1.

33. *Lumen Gentium*, §8. See also *Unitatis Redintegratio*.

and men holy and to save them, not as individuals without any bond between them, but rather to make them into a people who might acknowledge him and serve him in holiness."[34] It is for this reason that God elected Israel and established a covenant with them. God promised, through the prophet Jeremiah, to make a new covenant with the house of Judah, and Christ instituted this covenant in his blood, calling together a community made up of Jew and Gentile, consisting of people from all over the world.[35]

The church, as the holy people of God, shares in Christ's threefold office. As our High Priest and King, Jesus establishes the church as "a chosen people, a royal priesthood, a holy nation, God's special possession" (1 Pet 2:9). And while *Lumen Gentium* still argues that common priesthood and ministerial/hierarchical priesthood differ "essentially and not only in degree," it argues that "each in its own way shares in the one priesthood of Christ."[36] In this assertion, we see certain commonalities with the Reformation emphasis upon the priesthood of all believers. The church also shares in Christ's prophetic office, as "it spreads abroad a living witness to him, especially by a life of faith and love and by offering to God a sacrifice of praise, the fruit of lips confessing his name."[37] Also, as Christ had been sent by the Father, he sends the church into the world to "make disciples of all nations" (Matt 28:18)—to "be my witnesses in Jerusalem, in all Judea and Samaria, and to the ends of the earth" (Acts 1:8).[38]

---

34. *Lumen Gentium*, §9.
35. *Lumen Gentium*, §§9, 13.
36. *Lumen Gentium*, §10.
37. *Lumen Gentium*, §11.
38. *Lumen Gentium*, §17.

Lumen Gentium shows that the church cannot be reduced to the "institution," as though lay people are not also part of the church, or as though they are only "passive recipients of the ministrations and guidance of the clergy."[39] *Lumen Gentium* even devotes chapter 4 to the laity and argues in chapter 5 that "all in the church, whether they belong to the hierarchy or are cared for by it, are called to holiness."[40] It notes not only that the church is a pilgrim people, but it is a historical body "journeying from one epoch to another and one culture to another," and thus cannot be seen as "immutable or changeless."[41] One also cannot view the church as having already reached the end of its pilgrimage. While *Lumen Gentium* does not go so far as to say that the church has sinned, it says, "While Christ, holy, innocent and undefiled knew nothing of sin, but came to expiate only the sins of the people, the Church, embracing in its bosom sinners, at the same time holy and always in need of being purified, always follows the way of penance and renewal."[42] It also affirms that the church is "wounded by their sins"[43] and "exhorts her children to purification and renewal so that the sign of Christ may shine more brightly over the face of the earth."[44]

Service

As mentioned above, Lindbeck further breaks down his discussion of church and mission by addressing service,

---

39. *Lumen Gentium*, §30; cf. §§33–34.
40. *Lumen Gentium*, §39.
41. *Lumen Gentium*, §34.
42. *Lumen Gentium*, §8.
43. *Lumen Gentium*, §11.
44. *Lumen Gentium*, §15.

liturgy, communal unity, and common faith. Lindbeck says, "Because the function of the church in all aspects of its life and action is to point to the kingdom of love and justice which has come and is coming, its concrete service of mankind is no less integral a part of its mission and its witness than are its preaching, worship, and communal life."[45] So service can function as a "full anticipatory sign of the New Age," and that is the case because of the this-worldly character of the resurrection and consummation of all things.[46] The Council argues that the church should engage in secular service "because this constitutes a kind of pre-evangelization which contributes to the Christianization of the world and the ultimate triumph of the church."[47] It acknowledges that God is working in the world outside of the boundaries of the church and calls upon the church to "read the signs of the times"[48] and seek to "discern and contribute to what God is doing in history."[49] It should do so not in order to lord over the world, but because the church is a servant people—a nation on behalf of other nations.[50] As *Lumen Gentium* states, "the Church, although it needs human resources to carry out its mission, is not set up to seek earthly glory, but to proclaim, even by its own example, humility and self-sacrifice."[51] Lindbeck anticipates that there will be increased emphasis upon service in future Roman Catholic theology.

---

45. Lindbeck, *The Future of Roman Catholic Theology*, 38.
46. Lindbeck, *The Future of Roman Catholic Theology*, 38.
47. Lindbeck, *The Future of Roman Catholic Theology*, 43.
48. *Gaudium et Spes*, §4.
49. Lindbeck, *The Future of Roman Catholic Theology*, 47.
50. Lindbeck, *The Future of Roman Catholic Theology*, 48.
51. *Lumen Gentium*, §8.

GEORGE LINDBECK

Liturgy

While the Council places such an emphasis upon secular service, this does not mean that it neglects the church's liturgical practices—prayer, preaching, and the sacraments. Though Lindbeck raises concerns that the Council's emphasis upon service opened the way for some Catholics to minimize the liturgy and embrace a kind of "Christian secularism" already embraced by some Protestants,[52] *Sacrosanctum Concilium*, the Constitution on the Sacred Liturgy, argues that "the liturgy is the summit toward which the activity of the Church is directed; at the same time it is the font from which all her power flows."[53] In its worship, the church participates in the redemptive work of God in the world.

So, the church aims its life toward the worship and praise of God, and it is from the grace received in the liturgy, and in particular in the Eucharist, that acts of service flow.[54] Christians pray, preach, and worship because "they know they are called to witness to God's redemption, to be explicit witnesses and conscious bearers through all the

52. Lindbeck, *The Future of Roman Catholic Theology*, 52, 54–55.

53. *Sacrosanctum Concilium*, §10. *Lumen Gentium* similarly says that the Eucharistic sacrifice is "the source and summit of the christian life" (§11).

54. See *Lumen Gentium*, §33. Lindbeck notes, "This emphasis on worship as the dynamic source of good works has long been the standard view of most Christians, although they have differed as to exactly what kinds of liturgy are primary (individual or communal, eucharistic or non-eucharistic, formal or informal). Yet the correctness is questionable. Worship often does not lead to works, as St. Paul, not to mention the author of James, was well aware. Time and again the most assiduous cultivation of the sacraments, preaching, Bible-reading, prayer, and 'spiritual experiences' has been combined with flagrant moral and social irresponsibility" (Lindbeck, *The Future of Roman Catholic Theology*, 54).

ages of the memory and hope of the Messiah. They know they cannot do this without *leitourgia*, for memory and hope are rooted in liturgical action. Nor can they witness explicitly to all men without preaching to all."[55]

Lindbeck argues that this view of Christian witness is reminiscent of the role of Israel. He says, "All are called to the coming kingdom, but not all are called to bear witness to it."[56] The church is called to be a sign of and witness to Christ and the coming kingdom in every culture and country, but recognizes that it is not called to convert everyone. The church's primary concern should not be about numbers, but about whether or not it, as a community, faithfully witnesses to Christ. Lindbeck says, "It may be that it is only when the church is a smaller but more manifestly Christian anticipation of the love and unity of the coming kingdom that it will complete the task of meaningfully preaching and manifesting the gospel to all nations which the Bible tells us is a precondition for final redemption."[57]

In the liturgy of the word and of the sacrament, the church proclaims the mighty works of God, from the call of Abraham and the exodus from Egypt to those in the New Testament period, and argues that all these acts are summed up in the life, death, and resurrection of Jesus Christ.[58] Lindbeck says, "To participate in the liturgy is to participate in Christ's worship; it is for him to incorporate us into himself, part of the body."[59] This means that the sac-

---

55. Lindbeck, *The Future of Roman Catholic Theology*, 56.

56. Lindbeck, *The Future of Roman Catholic Theology*, 57.

57. Lindbeck, *The Future of Roman Catholic Theology*, 58. See Lindbeck, "The Sectarian Future."

58. Lindbeck, *The Future of Roman Catholic Theology*, 68–70.

59. Lindbeck, *The Future of Roman Catholic Theology*, 70.

rifice of the mass is not the church's meritorious work, but rather "Christ's own sacrifice of himself," and the church "joins believers to his sacrifice."[60]

Lindbeck then turns to other various concerns that Protestants have historically raised about Catholic worship for centuries. While not every liturgical abuse has been satisfactorily addressed, Vatican II began a process of practical reform. The liturgy is now in the vernacular and there is increased congregational participation, both in responses and hymn singing, and a greater emphasis upon the sermon. *Sacrosanctum Concilium* also opens up several other possibilities for liturgical reform, such as giving communion in both kinds (Luther's first captivity), the elimination of private masses, and permission for local adaptations. Lindbeck notes, however, that it may take decades for these reforms to take shape.[61] The Catholic liturgical movement also shares various features with non-Catholic liturgical renewal movements, such as the goal of restoring "the essential pattern or structure of Christian worship as this existed in the early centuries . . . in a form adapted to the present."[62] Also, because the Roman Catholic Church sees the church's worship as the work of Christ, *sola gratia*, the accusation of Protestants that the Roman Church argues that justification is by works or merit falls short.[63] While the Roman Catholic Church did not simply adopt Protestant positions, Lindbeck argues that in the Council's proclamations, many of the historic divisions between Protestants and Catholics are overcome.[64]

---

60. Lindbeck, *The Future of Roman Catholic Theology*, 71.
61. Lindbeck, *The Future of Roman Catholic Theology*, 63–64.
62. Lindbeck, *The Future of Roman Catholic Theology*, 62.
63. Lindbeck, *The Future of Roman Catholic Theology*, 71.
64. Lindbeck, *The Future of Roman Catholic Theology*, 58, 72.

Communal Unity

Lindbeck then turns to a discussion of the church's *koinonia*, its "character as a community of unifying love."[65] In this, Lindbeck focuses upon the manifestation or the visibility of *koinonia*, and he does so by looking at the Council's treatment of ecumenism and church structures.

Within a classical framework, whether Catholic or Protestant, that views the church as primarily proclaiming or mediating grace, there is no imperative for the church to maintain visible unity. Within the new vision of the world, one that shares a "realistically eschatological framework," Lindbeck observes, the church is called to be a sign of the coming kingdom:

> The church is to show that grace is precisely the reconciliation and the unification of all things in Christ. It thus becomes obvious that Christians must be reconciled among themselves and also be reconcilers in the world if they are to be credible and persuasive witnesses; if their witness is to prepare the world for that reconciliation which is in Christ, they must remind men of the true shape of the future which God wills for humanity. The ecumenical endeavor to manifest visibly the unity of all Christians is fundamental to the church's nature as sign and instrument of the eschatological unity of the divided world.[66]

Again, Lindbeck points to the first paragraph of *Lumen Gentium*, which depicts the church as "a sacrament—a sign and instrument, that is, of communion with God and the unity of the entire human race."[67] The paragraph then goes

---

65. Lindbeck, *The Future of Roman Catholic Theology*, 77.
66. Lindbeck, *The Future of Roman Catholic Theology*, 80.
67. *Lumen Gentium*, §1.

on to say, "The present situation lends greater urgency to this duty of the church, so that all people, who nowadays are drawn ever more closely together by social, technical and cultural bonds, may achieve full unity in Christ."[68] The Council also notes that the disunity of Christians "openly contradicts the will of Christ, scandalizes the world, and damages the sacred cause of preaching the Gospel to every creature."[69]

This proclamation signals a real shift in Catholic teaching. Some Protestants deny this, arguing that the ultimate object, for the Roman Catholic Church, is still an "ecumenism of return." While even *avant garde* Catholic theologians acknowledge the goal of institutional unity, this critique ignores the genuine changes in church teaching. As one example, Lindbeck notes that previous Catholic views on ecumenism "avoided preliminary and partial manifestations of unity on the grounds that these made it less apparent that Rome alone is the one true church."[70] The Roman Church previously discouraged ecumenical participation partly due to an emphasis upon returning to Rome, going so far as to call ecumenism "diabolical."[71]

Unitatis Redintegratio, the Second Vatican Council's Decree on Ecumenism, begins by saying, "The restoration of unity among all Christians is one of the principal concerns of the Second Vatican Council."[72] It recognizes that the ecumenical movement is the work of the Spirit, and that those who participate in it proclaim the Triune God. The Council even sees preliminary steps as "important in

68. *Lumen Gentium*, §1.
69. *Unitatis Redintegratio*, §1.
70. Lindbeck, *The Future of Roman Catholic Theology*, 81.
71. Lindbeck, *The Future of Roman Catholic Theology*, 82.
72. *Unitatis Redintegratio*, §1.

and of themselves even if they do not lead to full church unity."[73] For example, *Unitatis Redintegratio*, the Decree on Ecumenism, declares,

> Before the whole world let all Christians confess their faith in God, one and three, in the incarnate Son of God, our Redeemer and Lord. United in their efforts, and with mutual respect, let them bear witness to our common hope which does not play us false . . . Cooperation among Christians vividly expresses that bond which already unites them, and it sets in clearer relief the features of Christ the Servant . . . Through such cooperation, all believers in Christ are able to learn easily how they can understand each other better and esteem each other more, and how the road to the unity of Christians may be made smooth.[74]

Lindbeck then turns to the claim that the Roman Catholic Church is the one, true church, which leads many Protestants to conclude that ecumenical dialogue with the Roman Catholic Church is impossible. This may indeed have been true in the previous interpretation, in which other Christian communities, except perhaps for the Eastern Orthodox, are not churches at all, but false communities. Such is no longer the case according to Lindbeck: "the claim to be the one true church tends more and more to be limited to the single point that the Roman Church communion alone has *all* the institutional elements willed by Christ for his church,"[75] including the Petrine office. As *Lumen Gentium* famously argues, "This church, constituted and organized as a society in the present world, subsists in

73. Lindbeck, *The Future of Roman Catholic Theology*, 81.
74. *Unitatis Redintegratio*, §12.
75. Lindbeck, *The Future of Roman Catholic Theology*, 83.

the Catholic Church, which is governed by the successor of Peter and by the bishops in communion with him."[76]

The Council also recognizes, however, that other churches have several of these elements, such as the Bible, the liturgy, sacraments, and a regular ministry, as well as the gift and gifts of the Spirit. As *Unitatis Redintegratio* says,

> Catholics must gladly acknowledge and esteem the truly christian endowments from our common heritage which are to be found among those separated from us. It is right and salutary to recognize the riches of Christ and virtuous works in the lives of others who are bearing witness to Christ, sometimes even to the shedding of their blood.
>
> Nor should we forget that anything wrought by the grace of the holy Spirit in the hearts of our separated brothers and sisters can contribute to our own edification. Whatever is truly christian is never contrary to what genuinely belongs to the faith; indeed, it can always bring a more perfect realization of the very mystery of Christ and the church.[77]

Lindbeck notes that already in the few years after the end of the Council that the Roman Catholic Church became more active in ecumenical dialogue and cooperation than many churches who had been involved in the ecumenical movement for decades.[78]

---

76. *Lumen Gentium*, §8. Lindbeck argues that the fact that the document says "subsists in" rather than "is" provides the basis for ecumenical dialogue in *Unitatis Redintegratio*.

77. *Unitatis Redintegratio*, §4. In §§14–23, the document discusses this in relation to Orthodox and Protestant churches. I will return to this section of the document in the next chapter.

78. Lindbeck, *The Future of Roman Catholic Theology*, 84.

Lindbeck then turns to a discussion of church structures. Within the classical picture of the church, Lindbeck argues, the church is a hierarchical institution in which power and grace flow from the papacy to the bishops and priests and down to the passive laity. In contrast to this view, there is an "emerging vision of the messianic pilgrim people which gains its communal identity through worship. Where this concept is taken seriously, it is above all the laity, the *laos*, which is the church."[79] The clergy, in this view, are "the servants of the servants of God" that seek to "equip and aid the people in their service, witness, and worship."[80] This view thus emphasizes the collegiality of the whole church.

Lindbeck contends that this view can be seen in the documents of Vatican II, but "only obscurely and partially, even in the doctrinally basic third chapter of the Constitution of the Church, where the doctrine of episcopal collegiality is expounded."[81] When one looks at chapter 3 of *Lumen Gentium*, there is a discussion of collegiality, but it is relegated to the bishops. Also, he raises a concern that within this chapter, "the church as the body of Christ and the people of God is somehow secondary, a product of ecclesial institution."[82]

Despite this, Lindbeck argues that if one looks at the first two chapters—on the mystery of the church and the church as the people of God—as the center of *Lumen Gentium*, then one can see a different picture of the church. He says, "If one focuses on the church as the people of

79. Lindbeck, *The Future of Roman Catholic Theology*, 85.

80. Lindbeck, *The Future of Roman Catholic Theology*, 86. Popes have, since Pope Gregory I, identified themselves as *servus servorum Dei*, "the servant of the servants of God."

81. Lindbeck, *The Future of Roman Catholic Theology*, 86.

82. Lindbeck, *The Future of Roman Catholic Theology*, 87.

God in which, as the fourth chapter on the laity suggests, even the lowliest member has the right and responsibility to make his voice heard [§39], then it becomes natural to think of the entire company of Christians, and not simply the hierarchy, as collegially structured."[83] This should then lead to a greater level of participation by all members of the church, even in areas related to church government and doctrine. There should be a greater emphasis upon the *sensus fidelium* ("the sense of the faithful").

Pointing to the work of scholars like Hans Küng and Karl Rahner, Lindbeck argues that there may be a possibility of ecumenical agreement between Protestants and Catholics on the ministry of word and sacrament.[84] This is possible because "there is fundamental agreement on the divinely ordained (*de iure divino*) character of the office. The Reformers also insisted that it is given to the church by God."[85] He also believes there are grounds for an agreement on episcopacy. He points to the Apology of the Augsburg Confession, which expresses, "a 'deep desire to maintain' the historic episcopacy 'provided that the bishops stop raging against our churches.'"[86] After all, the Reformers saw their creation of separate orders as "an emergency measure which they hoped would be temporary."[87]

There is more difficulty for reconciliation on issues related to the papacy. He says, "The new perspectives favor reforming the papal office so that it would lose its unilaterally authoritarian features and become an institutional

---

83. Lindbeck, *The Future of Roman Catholic Theology*, 87.
84. See also Lindbeck, "Karl Rahner."
85. Lindbeck, *The Future of Roman Catholic Theology*, 88.
86. Lindbeck, *The Future of Roman Catholic Theology*, 89.
87. Lindbeck, *The Future of Roman Catholic Theology*, 89.

means not of monarchial ruling but of collegially preserving the visible unity of the universal church."[88] He argues that this would make the papacy acceptable to various Protestants, but it would not be acceptable to Catholics who argue that "it is a matter of divine law, not simply historical development, that this center of unity should be the Petrine See."[89] He does note, however, that some Catholic theologians have argued that due to changing circumstances, a reform of the papal office is necessary.[90] One could, Lindbeck proposes, argue that the papacy is a divine office in a way that is analogous to the Israelite monarchy (see First Samuel 8). It arose due to various historical circumstances and the demand of the people of Israel, but God assented to it. "[God] reluctantly approved an historical development resulting in part from the people's unfaithfulness. Perhaps in a similar way the successors of the apostle Peter, like the successors of King David in the days of old, have a place in the church by what might be called divine as well as human institution."[91] The Roman Catholic Church, however, may have difficulty arguing that the church has ever erred in such a way. Also, Protestantism depends for its existence on recognizing the legitimacy of its protest. They should, however, take the reforms of the Second Vatican Council seriously.[92]

---

88. Lindbeck, *The Future of Roman Catholic Theology*, 90.

89. Lindbeck, *The Future of Roman Catholic Theology*, 90.

90. Lindbeck, *The Future of Roman Catholic Theology*, 91–92.

91. Lindbeck, *The Future of Roman Catholic Theology*, 94.

92. See Lindbeck, "Papacy" for a more thorough treatment of these issues.

GEORGE LINDBECK

Common Faith

Lindbeck argues that the greatest obstacle to Christian unity is not ecclesial structures or the papacy, but debates related to the norm of the church's life. Should the church affirm the infallibility of the papacy or the magisterium or the Protestant principle of *sola Scriptura*? Both Protestants and Catholics agree that God's revelation culminates in the person and work of Jesus Christ, but they have historically answered this question, and related ones, in different ways. Lindbeck sees a path forward: "To the extent that Catholics and Protestants are able to recognize each other as genuinely striving to be faithful to the same Lord, to the Christ testified to in the Bible, they will find it possible to join forces as signs and agents of reconciliation in the world."[93] He then proceeds to re-evaluate the evangelical renewal in Roman Catholic thought he discussed in "Roman Catholicism on the Eve of the Council."

Lindbeck argues that because of the new vision of the world and the church, there has been a shift in Catholic perspectives on dogmatic infallibility. Previously, revelation was described as unchanging, eternal propositions. Various historical studies of the history of Christian thought have made various scholars, both Catholics and non-Catholics, aware of "the time-conditioned and culture-conditioned character of all human language, even when it is used by the church."[94] They have come to recognize that meaning changes depending upon the context.

This shift in understanding can be seen in *Dei Verbum*, the Dogmatic Constitution on Divine Revelation. In it, the Council argues that God sought to reveal Godself in order

---

93. Lindbeck, *The Future of Roman Catholic Theology*, 97.
94. Lindbeck, *The Future of Roman Catholic Theology*, 99.

to "invite and receive [humanity] into his company."[95] This revelation is not merely propositional, for

> The pattern of this revelation unfolds through deeds and words which are intrinsically connected: the works performed by God in the history of salvation show forth and confirm the doctrine and realities signified by the words; the words, for their part, proclaim the works, and bring to light the mystery they contain. The most important intimate truth thus revealed about God and human salvation shines forth for us in Christ, who is himself both the mediator and the sum total of revelation.[96]

It then goes on to reiterate that this revelation can be seen above all in "his death and glorious resurrection from the dead, and finally his sending of the Spirit of truth. He revealed that God was with us, to deliver us from the darkness of sin and death, and to raise us up to eternal life."[97]

This shift opens up the possibility of the reform of dogma and of the concept of infallibility. Because revelation centers upon events rather than propositions, dogmas "must be understood as necessarily inadequate and partial efforts to understand and interpret the mysteries of faith."[98] Lindbeck notes Catholic theologians, like Karl Rahner and Walter Kasper, have recognized this. As *Unitatis Redintegratio* says, "Consequently, if, in various times and circumstances, there have been deficiencies in moral conduct or in church discipline, or even in the way church teaching has been formulated—to be carefully distinguished from

95. *Dei Verbum*, §2.
96. *Dei Verbum*, §2.
97. *Dei Verbum*, §4.
98. Lindbeck, *The Future of Roman Catholic Theology*, 100.

the deposit of faith itself—these should be set right at the opportune moment and in the proper way."[99] Lindbeck argues that the church's understanding of the faith "needs to be constantly reformulated and corrected in light of changing circumstances and renewed attention to the sources of the faith."[100]

Lindbeck then turns to a discussion of *sola Scriptura*. He notes that this issue is important to Protestants because it is possible, "as various kinds of sectarians and theological liberals have done, to reject dogmatic and magisterial authority without becoming more biblical."[101] He argues that some of the developments of the Council "have been

---

99. *Unitatis Redintegratio*, §6.

100. Lindbeck, *The Future of Roman Catholic Theology*, 101. Lindbeck reiterates that the Council did not jettison the concept of infallibility. He says, "In short, the church must be able to make binding decisions on questions which threaten its unity, and these decisions are never so inadequate that they must be rejected, but they are in no sense sacrosanct supplements to revealed truth and are subject to constant review, supplementation, and interpretation" (105). He argues this view is similar to what the Orthodox and some Protestants would call the "indefectibility" of the church. He notes, however, that the view of the development of doctrine within the Council's documents differs from his own. They adhere more closely to John Henry Newman's organic theory of doctrinal development (101–2). He argues, however, that "the actions of the Council point in the direction of what we are calling the decision theory" (102). As an example, he points to *Dignitatis Humanae*, the Declaration on Religious Liberty, which reversed previous Catholic teaching on various issues. See also "Protestant Problems." He also authored several essays on infallibility during the Council and during the later Lutheran-Catholic dialogues. See "Reform and Infallibility," his essay in *The Infallibility Debate*, *Infallibility*, and "Problems." Lindbeck continues to advocate for this "'decision theory' of doctrine development" in *The Nature of Doctrine* (84–94).

101. Lindbeck, *The Future of Roman Catholic Theology*, 108.

in the direction of *sola Scriptura*."¹⁰² Some have added to this slogan the words *in ora ecclesiae*, but Lindbeck notes that this should not be an issue for Protestants. He says, "The so-called 'right to private interpretation' has no place in the central Reformation tradition. Scripture should always be read and interpreted in the community of believers."¹⁰³

This does not mean, however, that Protestants and Catholics use the slogan *sola Scriptura* in the same ways, but it is sometimes difficult to neatly differentiate between them. Some previously distinguished Protestant and Catholic views by saying Protestants affirm "Scripture alone," while Catholics look to "Scripture and tradition," but it is not so simple. He notes that Catholics typically speak about the "material sufficiency" of Scripture, and they do not see tradition as a second source but as "the medium in and through which the truths witnessed by the Bible are transmitted and interpreted."¹⁰⁴ They affirm the normativity of Scripture—that it is *norma normans, non normata* ("the norm of norms that cannot be normed"). Lindbeck argues that *Dei Verbum* was written somewhat ambiguously so that it is not always clear whether it is affirming a one-source or two-source theory of revelation, but it lends itself to such a one-source view.

This view is similar to one held by various Protestants, though Protestants sometimes raise questions about whether one can reconcile this view of Scripture with magisterial infallibility. Despite these concerns, Lindbeck argues that this shift is a real and important one, and that it also impacts the scholarship of those Catholics who accept

102. Lindbeck, *The Future of Roman Catholic Theology*, 108.
103. Lindbeck, *The Future of Roman Catholic Theology*, 109.
104. Lindbeck, *The Future of Roman Catholic Theology*, 109.

it. They are able to understand dogmas, such as Marian ones, in the light of Scripture in such a way that the Reformers could have understood them as pious opinions.[105] He also says, "It is safe to predict that the present trend toward increasing reliance on the Bible will continue in Roman Catholic theology."[106] And because various Catholic scholars, as well as the Council itself, have come to endorse historical-critical tools of studying the Bible, various convergences between Protestant and Catholic scholars have occurred, which is ecumenically promising.[107]

CONCLUSION

Lindbeck concludes *The Future of Roman Catholic Theology* by arguing, "The Council has opened up immense possibilities for the growing together of the Christian family, but whether they are actualized, and how they are actualized, depends on the collaboration of all the confessions."[108] He is not naively optimistic. He notes that various changes must take place before any large-scale reunion would be possible. But coming out of his experience as an observer at Vatican II, Lindbeck initially maintains a cautious optimism.

One can see a shift in his thought beginning with his 1975 essay, "The Crisis in American Catholicism."[109] Lindbeck argues that on the eve of the Second Vatican Council, American Catholicism "was more flourishing than it had

105. Lindbeck, *The Future of Roman Catholic Theology*, 111.
106. Lindbeck, *The Future of Roman Catholic Theology*, 112.
107. Lindbeck, *The Future of Roman Catholic Theology*, 113.
108. Lindbeck, *The Future of Roman Catholic Theology*, 118.
109. Bruce Marshall and Bernhard Eckerstorfer both see this essay as representative of a shift in Lindbeck's thought. See Marshall, "Introduction," x–xi; Eckerstorfer, "The One Church," 407–8.

ever been."[110] For the first time in American history, the president was a Roman Catholic and various Hollywood films centered upon Roman Catholic characters. The *aggiornamento*, the "updating," of the Second Vatican Council was praised not only by Catholics but by Protestants and even secularists. Various people, including Protestant observers, "forecast a great upsurge of Christian vitality and faithfulness within the Roman Catholic communion."[111] Lindbeck then concludes,

> What has happened, however, is in many ways the reverse of this. The aftermath of Vatican II can be read as disastrous. Piety, at least in its more visible forms, has declined. Even the older generation now goes to church less frequently, and younger American Catholics, according to the most recent statistics, are no more faithful in attendance than their Protestant counterparts. Catholic schools, after reaching their high point a decade ago, are now rapidly contracting. Priestly and religious vocations have dropped drastically in quantity and, some say, in quality also. Further, the tiny trickle of those leaving their churchly callings a decade ago has now grown to a torrent. Unless the loss in manpower and womanpower is sharply reversed, the collapse of traditional institutional forms will be inescapable in a few decades.
>
> In addition, the Church that was once a paragon of apparent peace and obedience is now wracked by open dissension.[112]

---

110. Lindbeck, "Crisis," 48.
111. Lindbeck, "Crisis," 49.
112. Lindbeck, "Crisis," 49.

He points, for example, to the conflicts surrounding the ban on birth control, priestly celibacy, intercommunion, women's ordination, infallibility, Vietnam, civil rights, and liberation theology.

The church has received the Council in cacophonous ways, largely because of the ambiguity of the Council documents. People across the spectrum can point to various texts to support their position. The Catholic Church is no longer growing as it once did, and various forms of popular piety are disappearing. In addition, while the Baltimore Catechism had previously provided a sense of what the Catholic Church affirms, shifts in how the church practices catechesis have produced a sense of confusion. So, in the short term, the picture looks grim. In the long term, however, the reforms of Vatican II may produce a leaner, more faithful church. Crises produce not only threats but opportunities, and so the crisis in the Catholic Church may lead to unforeseen and unexpected forms of life.[113]

Discussion Questions

1. What does it mean for there to be a genuine "evangelical revival" in the Roman Catholic Church?
2. How should one relate the two contrasting tendencies Lindbeck observed in the Roman Catholic Church: the evangelical revival and the contrasting emphasis upon Marian dogmas? Do we continue to see both tendencies in contemporary Roman Catholicism?
3. Lindbeck anticipated that the newer emphases in the Council documents would be the most significant for

---

113. Lindbeck, "Crisis," 56–66.

the future developments in Catholic Church. Has this been the case?

4. How does Lindbeck relate the new vision of the world to the new vision of the church and mission?

5. *Lumen Gentium* says that the church "subsists in the Catholic Church." What does this mean, and how does it relate to the increased emphasis upon ecumenism in the Roman Catholic Church?

6. How do Catholic and Protestant views of Scripture relate to one another?

5

ECUMENIST

LINDBECK PARTICIPATED IN SOME ecumenical dialogues prior to his role as an observer during Vatican II, but in the years after the Council, his participation increased. He participated mostly in Lutheran-Catholic dialogue, on a national and international level, and even served during the 1970s and 1980s as co-chair of the Lutheran World Federation/Vatican Joint Study Commission.[1] This chapter surveys Lindbeck's view of ecumenical dialogue before focusing upon his work on justification.

DOCTRINAL RECONCILIATION WITHOUT CAPITULATION

Lindbeck emphasized doctrinal reconciliation without capitulation, saying, "The unity of the churches is not properly attained by surrender, capitulation, or loss of

---

1. Lindbeck, *The Nature of Doctrine*, xxix. For a list of the dialogues Lindbeck participated in, see "Writings," 297–98.

identity on any side."[2] Lindbeck argues this emphasis is not only present within Protestant ecumenical circles, but within Catholic circles as well. This can be seen in *Unitatis Redintegratio*, the Second Vatican Council's document on ecumenism—particularly in its treatment of the Eastern Orthodox. The writers of the document recognize the unique contribution the churches of the East have made to the liturgy and theology of the Roman Catholic Church, and call upon ecumenists to "give due consideration to this special feature of the origin and growth of the churches of the east."[3] The document later states that when the East and West understand doctrines differently, "these various theological formulations are often to be considered complementary rather than conflicting."[4]

For those churches in the West separate from Rome, *Unitatis Redintegratio* extends hope that "an ecumenical spirit and mutual esteem will gradually increase among all Christians."[5] It recognizes the differences present within various churches and "ecclesial communities," for "there are very weighty differences not only of a historical, sociological, psychological and cultural character," but also in "the interpretation of revealed truth."[6] They rejoice in knowing that there are "separated sisters and brothers" who "look to Christ as the source and center of ecclesiastical communion."[7] They also acknowledge a sacramental bond created through baptism, commonalities in liturgy

2. Lindbeck, *Infallibility*, 7.
3. *Unitatis Redintegratio*, §14.
4. *Unitatis Redintegratio*, §17.
5. *Unitatis Redintegratio*, §19.
6. *Unitatis Redintegratio*, §19.
7. *Unitatis Redintegratio*, §20.

and morality, and that the church's unity is ultimately a divine work.⁸

In his Père Marquette lectures, *Infallibility*, Lindbeck says that each Christian group must take their traditional positions seriously because "neglect of tradition is a major component in the sickness of our age."⁹ He continues, "Without tradition, without shared memories, there is no community; and without community, there is no firm personal identity for the individual."¹⁰ For the church to develop this communal consciousness, however, Christians must not only look at their own traditions, but at one another's traditions: "[T]he ability of the church to foster a sense of community and of personal identity depends on the preservation and enrichment of shared memories of all the communal and individual ways of being Christian which have developed in two thousand years of history."¹¹ Christians should not only study these traditions, but also see how they need to be "reformulated and reevaluated" without "destroying the resources available for what it is."¹²

---

8. *Unitatis Redintegratio*, §22–24.

9. Lindbeck, *Infallibility*, 9.

10. Lindbeck, *Infallibility*, 9. Lindbeck does not address this issue from a purely male, Eurocentric perspective. He notes, "This has been most recently discovered by both blacks and the women's liberation forces. They started with efforts to free the individual, that is, with new attempts to give blacks and women new and more fully human identities, a sense of clarity and pride about what it is to be a black or about what it is to be a women. They soon found, however, that in order to do this it is necessary to develop communal consciousness; and communal consciousness, in turn, requires a sense of tradition. The result has been a vast outpouring of historical and pseudo-historical writing about blacks and about women and their struggles for equality in the past" (9–10).

11. Lindbeck, *Infallibility*, 10.

12. Lindbeck, *Infallibility*, 10.

Lindbeck notes that both in general and in studying the doctrines and theologies of various Christian traditions, a logical contradiction is particularly difficult to demonstrate. As an example of this, Lindbeck points to Thomas Aquinas's discussion of language. Thomas says that when someone speaks of an animal and a picture of an animal, they are using the word "animal" equivocally. In similar way, Thomas says, "When [the heathen] says an idol is God, he does not signify the true Deity. On the other hand, a Catholic signifies the true Deity when he says that there is one God. Therefore this name *God* is not applied univocally, but equivocally to the true God, and to God according to that opinion."[13] Lindbeck also draws upon linguistic philosophy, as seen in Wittgenstein, which emphasizes that meaning is dependent upon use and function. Then, Lindbeck adds onto this the work of historians and cultural anthropologists who discuss "the mutability and pluralism of intellectual, religious, and psychosocial situations" and Bernard Lonergan's (1904–1984) argument that there are sixty-four distinct forms of consciousness, "each one of which alters meaning."[14] All of these streams further complexify the picture. Lindbeck says:

> The conclusion to be drawn is that when Catholics affirm and Protestants deny magisterial and dogmatic infallibility, they are almost certainly not speaking of the same thing and consequently are not contradicting each other in any precisely

---

13. Aquinas, *Summa Theologiae*, I.13.10. Thomas says below in the reply to objection 4, "The term *animal* applied to a true and a pictured animal is not purely equivocal; for the Philosopher takes equivocal names in a large sense, including analogous names; because also being, which is predicated analogically, is sometimes said to be predicated equivocally of different predicaments."

14. Lindbeck, *Infallibility*, 13.

specifiable sense. Consequently, although their positions are obviously very different, it is not absurd to ask whether they might be reconcilable within a new hermeneutical setting constituted by changes in theology, piety, institutional forms, and the church's situation in the world.[15]

Lindbeck carries on this perspective not only in his discussions of infallibility, but other issues as well.

Lindbeck does not approach this task naively. He admits that these traditions not only build community, but also divide communities. He acknowledges the difficulty of reconciling Protestants and Catholics on difficult issues like infallibility or justification.[16] While a contradiction is difficult to demonstrate, he argues as well that "reconcilability is also hard to demonstrate."[17] In this context, Lindbeck cites Karl Rahner, who argues that "the only proof of the compatibility of diverse doctrines is the establishment of communion between the churches that adhere to them."[18] Lindbeck sees an example of this communion in the unity of the New Testament canon, in which diverse theological claims are made but unified by the common faith attested therein.[19] He argues that Christians should not yield to the temptation of relevance—of simply forgetting the past and starting anew—or what he later calls "unmediated *aggiornamento*."[20] Instead, Christians should

15. Lindbeck, *Infallibility*, 13–14.

16. Lindbeck, *Infallibility*, 12.

17. Lindbeck, "A Question of Compatibility," 231.

18. Lindbeck, "A Question of Compatibility," 231.

19. Lindbeck, "A Question of Compatibility," 231.

20. Lindbeck, "Confession and Community," 494. *Aggiornamento* is a term used by Catholic theologians and clergy in the time of Vatican II to emphasize the need for the church to bring itself "up to date."

first look to these traditions and see if the various doctrines within them are in fact incompatible.

JUSTIFICATION

To exemplify how Lindbeck practices this ecumenical methodology, I will look at his approach to justification. Lindbeck's initial writing on justification came out of the seventh round of discussions between the Roman Catholic Bishops Committee for Ecumenical and Interreligious Affairs and the United States Committee of the Lutheran World Federation in the United States, which took place from 1978 to 1983 and concluded with a common statement.[21] This dialogue arose in the aftermath of the 1977 Lutheran World Federation Assembly at Dar-es-salaam, in which the assembly accepted the recommendation of some Lutheran and Catholic theologians that a discussion take place on the possible recognition of the Augsburg Confession by the Roman Catholic Church.[22]

Lindbeck presented four session papers during this period of US Lutheran-Catholic dialogue on justification: "Justification in the Catholic-Lutheran Dialogues and in Discussions of the Recognition of the Augsburg Confession" in September 1978, "Some Lutheran Reflections on Trent" in March 1980, "A Lutheran Approach to the Limits of Diversity in the Understanding

---

21. See Anderson et al., *Justification by Faith*; 8–12 give some background on the dialogues and the session papers that were presented. The statement is included on 13–74. See Lindbeck and Vajta, "The Augsburg Confession," 82; 93n1.

22. In a co-written essay, Lindbeck and Vilmos Vajta extend hope that the Lutheran-Catholic dialogues have helped the two churches come closer together, and also closer to the writers of the Augsburg Confession in 1530 (Lindbeck and Vajta, "The Augsburg Confession," 81).

of Justification" in September 1980, and "What's New About Our Statement?" in September 1982. Only two of the essays, the ones presented in 1980, have been published—the first in *Justification by Faith: Lutherans and Catholics in Dialogue VII,* and the second in *Lutheran Theological Seminary Bulletin.*[23]

These writings on justification principally engage the treatment of justification in the Augsburg Confession (1530) and the Council of Trent (1545–1563). Augsburg treats the doctrine of justification in chapter 4:

> It is also taught among us that we cannot obtain forgiveness of sin and righteousness before God by our own merits, works, or satisfactions, but that we receive forgiveness of sin and become righteous before God by grace, for Christ's sake, through faith, when we believe that Christ suffered for us and that for his sake our sin is forgiven and righteousness and eternal life are given to us. For God will regard and reckon this faith as righteousness, as Paul says in Romans 3:21–26 and 4:5.[24]

Trent treats justification much more extensively, including sixteen chapters and thirty-three canons. A few canons problematize the possible compatibility of Trent and Augsburg, but one particular canon of Trent demonstrates the difficulty of convergence—canon 9: "If anyone says that the sinner is justified by faith alone, meaning thereby that no other co-operation is required for him to obtain the grace of justification, and that in no sense is it necessary for

---

23. Anderson et al., *Justification by Faith*, 10–12.
24. *The Book of Concord*, 30.

him to make preparation and be disposed by a movement of his own will: let him be anathema."[25]

Lindbeck notes in these 1980 essays, presented nineteen years before the *Joint Declaration on the Doctrine of Justification*, "A suggestion that Tridentine and Lutheran confessional teaching on justification may be compatible is a modest one. To say that two positions are possibly compatible means no more than that they have not been proved contradictory."[26] In the first essay, later published as, "A Question of Compatibility: A Lutheran Reflects on Trent," Lindbeck says that the most difficult issue to address is whether or not the Tridentine and Lutheran confessions "anathematize each other," or instead, possibly in the case of something like canon 9, simply condemn caricatures of the Catholic and Lutheran positions. Another question raised is whether or not Trent's discussion of justification can be interpreted in such a way that Lutherans would not see it as heretical.[27]

This second question is particularly important, for while in Lutheran–Roman Catholic dialogue the Catholics are often the ones unable to "maneuver" due to various traditions and church pronouncements, on the issue of justification the Lutherans have less room for flexibility

---

25. Tanner, *Decrees*, 679. For other examples, see also canons 12 and 24.

26. Lindbeck, "A Question," 230. See above discussion of contradiction. Lindbeck focuses primarily within these pieces on the relationship of Trent to the Lutheran Confessions rather than to Luther himself. He says, "Luther's theology, to be sure, is for most purposes more important than the official Lutheranism of the *Book of Concord*, just as Augustine's thought is more important than the official Augustinianism of the Synod of Orange. Ecclesiastically authoritative doctrine does at times need to be considered, however, and this dialogue is one of those occasions" (232).

27. Lindbeck, "A Question," 231.

because they have historically considered the doctrine of justification by faith alone (*sola fide*) as *articulus stantis et cadentis ecclesiae,* "the article on which the church stands and falls." For example, Lindbeck's fellow Lutheran ecumenist Robert Jenson remains skeptical of the compatibility of Lutheran and traditional Catholic perspectives on justification.[28]

Lindbeck lays out how certain terms were used among the Tridentine and Lutheran writers in the sixteenth century. It is commonly understood that Trent defines faith in an "intellectualist" way while the Lutherans understand faith as "fiducial." Lindbeck addresses this discussion under three points:

> For the purposes of this essay it is assumed that Roman Catholics are right when they argue (1) that Trent could have combined *assensus* and *fiducia* in its concept of faith and (2) that this would have made it possible to affirm that justification is in one sense *sola fide* . . . In this essay it is also assumed that those are right who argue (3) that Luther's certitude of faith and the certitude of hope affirmed in the Roman Catholic tradition do not exclude each other.[29]

Lindbeck notes that while these three points do not constitute agreement between Trent and the Lutheran confessions, they together make it difficult to see the understandings of faith as "mutually exclusive affirmations about the nature and role of faith."[30] Both understandings

---

28. Lindbeck, "Article IV," 3. See Jenson, "On Recognizing," 151–66.

29. Lindbeck, "A Question," 233.

30. Lindbeck, "A Question," 233.

of faith emphasize that humans are dependent upon God alone for salvation.

While Lindbeck has optimism about a possible convergence on the definition of faith, he sees difficulty in a convergence on the sinfulness and righteousness of Christians. This can be seen in three mutually related topics: (1) whether or not concupiscence is sin, (2) the acceptance or rejection of *simul iustus et peccator*, and (3) the inherent righteousness of the Christian. He notes concerning the first,

> In reference to sin it is relatively easy to argue for doctrinal compatibility (not, be it noted, agreement) between Trent and the Reformation on the status in the justified of the concupiscence which afflicts all those born in original sin, but more difficult to argue for doctrinal compatibility when one takes *simul iustus et peccator* into consideration.[31]

Lindbeck notes that a convergence on the first half of the above statement was possible even in the sixteenth-century context. Both assumed three things about concupiscence after baptism: "(1) [it] is from sin, inclines to sin, and must be constantly and stoutly resisted even though (2) it no longer dominates or alienates from God as it does in the unjustified, and (3) it is forgiven."[32] While Catholics at Augsburg in 1530 accepted the idea that concupiscence is sin, those at Trent did not.[33] Some contemporary thinkers,

31. Lindbeck, "A Question," 233.

32. Lindbeck, "A Question," 233.

33. Lindbeck, "A Question," 234. Lindbeck notes that Trent's definitions of such matters are complicated due to the controversies that developed there. He argues that Trent "adopted the definition that embraced the widest possible range of Roman Catholic teachings ... Thus some of the understandings of concupiscence and original

like Lutheran Edmund Schlink and Roman Catholic Otto Pesch (1931–2014), have sought to resolve these tensions. Lindbeck summarizes their solution saying, "The Reformational way of speaking, one can argue, is appropriate in a penitential context, while the Tridentine recommendation fits a doxological one."[34] Thus from one perspective, the penitential one, a person must ask God for forgiveness from all that contradicts God's will, including sinful desires, while from the other perspective, one must praise God for freedom from bondage to sin. Lindbeck notes that this perspective lines up with the view of Philip Melanchthon, who argues that "whether concupiscence is properly sin depends on the 'place' of speaking."[35]

In regards to the acceptance or rejection of *simul iustus et peccator*, Lindbeck argues the real challenge comes in the interpretation canon 25 in Trent's discussion of justification. The canon says, "If anyone says that in any good work a just person sins at least venially, or (which is more intolerable) mortally, and thus deserves eternal punishments, and is not thereby damned only because God does not impute those works unto damnation: let him be anathema."[36] Lindbeck notes in response to this canon, "These words are not *ipsissima verba* [the very words] to be found in the Lutheran Confessions, but there is no doubt that what is here condemned is so deeply embedded in Luther and Lutheran theology that it has the force of official doctrine."[37] Lindbeck thus concludes that this

---

sin represented at Trent may have been compatible with those of the Reformers, while others were not."

34. Lindbeck, "A Question," 234.
35. Lindbeck, "A Question," 234.
36. Tanner, *Decrees*, 680.
37. Lindbeck, "A Question," 235.

difference cannot simply be seen as a "verbal difference." As he notes, "The Reformers claim that all human actions need forgiveness, while Trent denies this."[38]

Again, however, Lindbeck claims that one can look to this difference as a matter of perspective. He notes that for Luther, even the "best deed of the best person" is not without sin, and so every person is in need of mercy. Luther saw this not as speculation but as scriptural. As Isaiah 64:6 says, "All our righteous deeds are like a filthy cloth." Luther did note, however, that times exist in which it is incorrect to say, "All our righteous deeds are like a filthy cloth." Luther saw a Tridentine emphasis on the removal of the sin of the justified as appropriate against those who deny or minimize the transforming power of grace, but argued against Trent that he was not one of those minimizers. Lindbeck notes that despite such claims, Luther did not argue for a "purely external or extrinsic imputation of righteousness" seen within some later Lutherans. Lindbeck thus concludes that canon 25 does not completely contradict the Lutheran emphasis upon *simul iustus et peccator*.[39]

Third, Trent argues in chapter 7 that justification "consists not only in the forgiveness of sins but also in the sanctification and renewal of the inward being by a willing acceptance of the grace and gifts whereby someone from being unjust becomes just, from being an enemy becomes a friend, so that he is an heir *in hope of eternal life*."[40] Lindbeck argues that while Lutherans agree that justification is not limited to the "nonimputation of sin" and that justification also entails the renewal of the justified, Lutherans make this argument apart from the language of inherent

---

38. Lindbeck, "A Question," 235.
39. Lindbeck, "A Question," 236.
40. Tanner, *Decrees of the Ecumenical Council*, 673.

righteousness: "They do not talk of the transformation of the old self by the infusion of grace, but are more likely to speak in terms of the gift, birth, or creation of a new self. The redeemed self is discontinuous with the old."[41] So both Trent and Augsburg affirm the genuine renewal of the believer, but they do so in different ways. Luther, in particular, denied "the Scholastic notion of grace as a habit or disposition of the soul," which he deemed as a corruption from Aristotelian philosophy.[42] This debate can be seen as revolving around whether or not infusion of righteousness is wholly the work of God, or also includes a contribution from the human.

Lindbeck notes that some contemporary Catholics, like Rahner and Edward Schillebeeckx (1914–2009), utilize patristic and Eastern notions of divinization to resolve this dilemma and make "inherent righteousness . . . totally and continuously dependent on uncreated grace, on God himself."[43] Lindbeck sees this solution as compatible with Reformation insights and possibly also with Thomas Aquinas, but does not see it as congruent with Trent, for Trent discusses inherent righteousness as "the *causa formalis* of justification in the specific sense that the justified 'may bear it before the tribunal of our Lord Jesus Christ and may have life eternal.'"[44] Within this understanding of justification, no "alien righteousness," such as that given from God's mercy in Christ, is needed because "Eternal life is merited because of the goodness of good works."[45]

---

41. Lindbeck, "A Question," 237.
42. Lindbeck, "A Question," 237.
43. Lindbeck, "A Question," 238.
44. Lindbeck, "A Question," 239. See Tanner, *Decrees*, 239.
45. Lindbeck, "A Question," 239.

Ecumenist

Lindbeck points to one scholar who offers a solution to this problem: Reinhard Koesters (1885–1956). Koesters argues that instead of seeing Trent as envisioning a two-fold judgment, one "on the way" and a second eschatological one, one should see "the initial transforming declaration of righteousness" as having "eschatological validity," for "when God accepts sinners, he does so definitively." One could thus see inherent righteousness as "the effect rather than the cause of God's pronouncements that this human being is just," and thus "the justified cannot appeal to it or rely upon it *coram deo* [in the presence of God]."[46] Lindbeck surmises that Luther would accept this solution.

In the second essay on justification, later published as "Article IV and Lutheran/Roman Catholic Dialogue: The Limits of Diversity in the Understanding of Justification," Lindbeck argues that the contemporary Catholic consensus is that "justification by faith as interpreted by contemporary Lutherans is not excluded by Catholic teaching."[47] Lindbeck also notes that Catholics today are not likely to defend abuses in worship and church practice connected with justification that are criticized within the Augsburg Confession.[48] Lindbeck proceeds to ask what the limits of acceptable diversity are for Lutherans, particularly because Lutheran rigidity on the issue of justification "seems strange not only to Roman Catholics but to most of our contemporaries."[49]

---

46. Lindbeck, "A Question," 239.

47. Lindbeck, "Article IV," 3. Lindbeck cites as evidence German language studies on the issue by Otto Hermann Pesch and Vinzenz Pfnur, and a Lutheran/Roman Catholic commentary on the Augsburg Confession (also German-language) (3n1).

48. Lindbeck, "Article IV," 13

49. Lindbeck, "Article IV," 3.

Lindbeck summarizes the difference between the Reformers and the Catholic tradition on justification by saying,

> For the Reformers, God accepts the unacceptable, while for the Catholic tradition, God first makes the unacceptable acceptable and then accepts them. For the Catholics in other words, God forgives only after first infusing the grace which enables sinners to do the works of love which merit salvation. These good works are, according to such *sola gratia* Catholics as Augustine and Thomas Aquinas, entirely from grace.[50]

Lindbeck notes that Luther and his colleagues recognized the strengths in those they referred to as "better scholastics." For instance, Luther's associate Philip Melanchthon cites Augustine in his *Apology* saying, "When God rewards our merits, it is his own gifts which he crowns."[51] Lutherans and Catholics thus have some similarity in their perspectives on justification. "Both groups could affirm human beings are by themselves utterly helpless in the face of sin or meaninglessness, and that they are utterly dependent on God for salvation."[52]

Lindbeck notes as well, however, that their positions also differ in various ways. The Catholic *sola gratia* perspective assumes the goodness of Christians. This goodness of Christians should not lead to pride, but instead reminds Christians that "they should attribute all their virtues and merits to God."[53] The Reformation position, however, as-

50. Lindbeck, "Article IV," 5.
51. As cited in Lindbeck, "Article IV," 5.
52. Lindbeck, "Article IV," 5.
53. Lindbeck, "Article IV," 5. Lindbeck is careful to note that this perspective does not assume the goodness of humanity apart from grace.

sumes that even Christians have a total absence of inherent goodness. Lindbeck summarizes these differences saying, "Luther and the Augsburg Confession emphasize faith or trust in opposition to despair, while Augustine and the Catholic councils stress humility and praise of God in opposition to pride."[54] The Reformers, in Lindbeck's perspective, saw the Catholic tradition as incapable of preventing despair. While they saw some strength in Augustine's *sola gratia* message in its anti-Pelagian context, they thought the message of *sola gratia* could lead to dangerous consequences in light of the medieval penitential tradition. Thus, the Reformers claimed that the only proper response was to preach justification by faith alone.

Lindbeck argues that to judge the acceptable limits of diversity, one needs a "metatheological rule"—a rule that can test various theologies of justification. He defines this further, saying, "A metatheological norm of justification does not supply a vision or theory of God's justifying action or of the reality of justification in human lives, but rather prescribes conditions which all such theologies of justification must meet."[55] For example, Lindbeck claims that when Lutherans declare that the doctrine of justification by faith is "the 'article on which the Church stands and falls,'" they are setting up a metatheological rule. Lindbeck proposes a particular sixteenth-century Lutheran rule as a metatheological guide for acceptable diversity in this instance: "all church teaching and practices should function to promote reliance or trust in the God of Jesus Christ alone for salvation."[56] This rule, in and of itself, does not

54. Lindbeck, "Article IV," 5.
55. Lindbeck, "Article IV," 6.
56. Lindbeck, "Article IV," 6.

give an explicit definition of justification, and Lindbeck does not seek to demonstrate at length the compatibility of this proposed rule with Luther and the Augsburg Confession, though he thinks such a compatibility is plausible. Rather, Lindbeck sees the historical questions as secondary and instead suggests, "It is enough for our purposes to simply stipulate that a theology or practice is tolerable to the extent that it can be used to promote, or at least not hinder, the communication of the reality of justifying faith—that is, faith which clings to God in Christ alone."[57] The closer a doctrine or practice adheres to this rule, the better it is.

Lindbeck then draws eight consequences from his rule. First, a focus upon his rule can make it easier to understand why so little discussion about justification by faith exists prior to the sixteenth century. Rules, Lindbeck argues, "can be followed in practice without any explicit or theoretical knowledge of them."[58] Second, "Just as skill in following a rule can exist without explicit knowledge of it, so knowledge can exist without skill."[59] Because of this, Lindbeck observes that many Lutherans know the rule of justification, but do not know how the rule should be applied in the lives of individual Christians or within the church, and "[s]ometimes, indeed, preoccupation with the rule of justification seems to make it more difficult to practice the reality, just as constant attention to the rules of correct fingering can make it impossible to play a sonata or type fifty words a minute."[60] Third, the second consequence does not make doctrine unimportant. Explicit

57. Lindbeck, "Article IV," 6.
58. Lindbeck, "Article IV," 7.
59. Lindbeck, "Article IV," 7.
60. Lindbeck, "Article IV," 7.

rules are particularly useful in catechesis and the teaching of the faith.

Fourth, Lindbeck notes that the primary conflict between Rome and Lutherans has not been over the metatheological rule, but over different theologies of justification. Lindbeck says, "Nowhere does the Tridentine decree, for example, specifically deny the metadoctrine."[61] Lindbeck points to times when it uses language similar to the rule. For example, in chapter 16, it says, "'*absit tamen, ut christianus homo in se ipso vel confidant vel glorietur et non in Domino*' ('far be it from a Christian to confide or glory in himself and not in the LORD')."[62] Also, while canon 32 speaks of merit as a condition for eternal life, chapter 9 argues that one cannot rely upon merit for salvation. Lindbeck says, "In short, while Trent does not assert reliance for justification on the God and Father of Jesus Christ alone, neither does it assert the contrary."[63]

Lindbeck notes fellow Lutherans like Gerhard Ebeling (1912–2001) and Robert Jenson disagree with him on this point. They see the Aristotelean or Platonic anthropology and metaphysics that Trent and similar Catholic doctrinal formulations are indebted to as contrary to the gospel and to the Reformation doctrine of justification by faith. Due to his indebtedness to certain streams of Anglo-American analytic philosophy, Lindbeck disagrees with their *a priori* arguments: "Metaphysical notions of substance and infused grace, for example, can be employed for many different purposes; and it is by no means clear that all of these are incompatible with the *sola fide*."[64] He also notes that

61. Lindbeck, "Article IV," 7.
62. Lindbeck, "Article IV," 7–8.
63. Lindbeck, "Article IV," 8.
64. Lindbeck, "Article IV," 8.

pre-Reformation theologies, as seen in Thomas Aquinas, are less polemical than post-Reformation theologies, and thus also less systematic. It is thus difficult to speculate on how someone like Thomas would have responded to the Reformation debates concerning justification.

Fifth, Lindbeck is also willing to relativize Luther's theology in light of the metatheological rule. He says, "The concepts and models which the Reformers employed are not normative in themselves, but only to the extent that they are necessary and effective to promote the communication of justifying faith."[65] Lindbeck sees this as particularly important to emphasize in light of various misuses of Luther and the Reformers.[66] Sixth, Lindbeck offers a qualified critique of certain Lutheran theologians for whom the task of systematic theology and the interpretation of Luther are a common task. Lindbeck says, "I do not deny the value of such contributions, but I question the view that a theology is Lutheran only if it uses a Reformation conceptuality."[67]

Seventh, Lindbeck argues that some contemporary traditions may follow the metatheological rule in a generally unconscious way. He still sees them as within the limit of acceptable diversity. Eighth, Lindbeck argues that study of Luther and the Reformation tradition actually becomes more important in light of his approach. The type of study that must be done, however, "becomes more difficult and demanding. We are called upon, not to repeat

65. Lindbeck, "Article IV," 9.

66. Lindbeck, "Article IV," 9–10. Among these misuses, Lindbeck mentions those who read Luther's understanding of justification by faith in an existentialist (as opposed to sapiential) direction.

67. Lindbeck, "Article IV," 11. Lindbeck connects his view of Luther again with his view that the Reformation is a reform movement within the universal church.

Luther, but to do with very different conceptual materials what he did with the ideas available in the 16th century... [Luther] frees us to follow his example rather than imitate his thought."[68]

In conclusion, Lindbeck argues that while an increasing number of Catholics no longer see justification by faith as antithetical to Catholic teaching, Lutherans should not dogmatically insist that Roman Catholics accept the "dogmatization of the *sola fide* as a condition of church fellowship."[69] Lutherans should instead ask "for 'the freedom of gospel.'"[70] Lindbeck claims that Lutherans would, in fact, "contradict their own *raison d'etre* if they demanded that others officially affirm the norm of justification *sola fide* as a pre-condition for unity."[71] Unity does not require uniformity.

CONCLUSION

Though still in a nascent form, a few insights in these earlier writings on justification can be seen in the 1984 book, *The Nature of Doctrine*. For example, Lindbeck distinguishes between first- and second-order language as well as doctrines/metatheological rules and theology, discusses the regulative role that doctrines play, and is working out his later understanding of a "cultural-linguistic" understanding of doctrine through his use of anthropologists like Clifford Geertz and philosophers like Ludwig Wittgenstein.

Within his writings on justification, Lindbeck offers a compelling, modest, and nuanced account of how

68. Lindbeck, "Article IV," 11.
69. Lindbeck, "Article IV," 13.
70. Lindbeck, "Article IV," 13.
71. Lindbeck, "Article IV," 13–14.

GEORGE LINDBECK

Catholics and Lutherans can be seen to share a compatible understanding that humans depend upon God's grace for justification and salvation. Lindbeck utilizes historical, sociological, and philosophical tools—for theological reasons—in order to propose such a noncontradiction. His work, as well as that of some of his Lutheran and Catholic ecumenical colleagues, also anticipates and prepares the way for the *Joint Declaration on the Doctrine of Justification* in 1999.[72]

Discussion Questions

1. Is doctrinal reconciliation without capitulation possible? If so, what are its limits?
2. How can we know when people do contradict one another?
3. What is faith? How did Catholics and Lutherans define faith in the sixteenth-century disputes?
4. Do both the Lutheran and Catholic views of justification meet the criteria for Lindbeck's metatheological rule that they should "promote reliance or trust in the God of Jesus Christ alone for salvation"? Is the rule that he proposes sufficient?
5. What level of uniformity is needed for unity?

---

72. Helmer, *How Luther*, 108. Helmer there says, "Lindbeck's ecumenical-theological proposal paved the way not only for the signing of the Joint Declaration on the Doctrine of Justification on October 31, 1999, but also inspired a generation of American Lutherans to approach Luther as a late medieval Catholic theologian."

6

POSTLIBERAL

LINDBECK SAYS THAT HE initially wrote *The Nature of Doctrine* in order to address his own growing dissatisfaction with how the doctrines and dogmas of the church are understood in ecumenical dialogues. He says, "It has become apparent to me, during twenty-five years of involvement in ecumenical discussions and in teaching the history and present status of doctrines, that those of us who are engaged in these activities lack adequate categories for conceptualizing the problems that arise."[1] This problem involves not only doctrines in isolation, but, he argues, "the notion of religion itself."[2] He contends that the solution is not simply to abandon all modern developments and return to a "preliberal orthodoxy." Instead, he says, "A third, a postliberal way of conceiving religion and religious doctrine is called for."[3] Here, Lindbeck coins the unhyphenated term "postliberal[ism]," and he uses it to

1. Lindbeck, *The Nature of Doctrine*, xxxiii.
2. Lindbeck, *The Nature of Doctrine*, xxxiii.
3. Lindbeck, *The Nature of Doctrine*, xxxiii.

distinguish this approach from various other approaches that could be called post-liberal.[4] This chapter begins with a summary of the ecumenical focus of the first five chapters of *The Nature of Doctrine* before turning to Lindbeck's discussion of postliberal theology.

INTRODUCTION TO THE NATURE OF DOCTRINE

Much of *The Nature of Doctrine* began with Lindbeck's St. Michael's Lectures at Gonzaga University in 1974.[5] Lindbeck clarifies that while the focus of the book is upon intra-Christian ecumenical issues, "the theory of religion and religious doctrine that it proposes is not specifically ecumenical, nor Christian, nor theological."[6] To develop it, he draws upon the work of various philosophical and social-scientific perspectives, and so it could help those who study religion for both nontheological and theological reasons. He argues that this is important because "[a] theory of religion and doctrine cannot be ecumenically useful unless it is nonecumenically plausible."[7] He thus argues that some could read it in order to come to a clearer understanding of religion and religious doctrine more broadly, but he primarily intends the book to serve as prolegomena to a work "on the current status of doctrinal agreements and disagreements of the major Christian traditions,"[8] a project he later abandoned.[9]

4. Lindbeck, "Introduction," xviiin10.

5. Lindbeck, *The Nature of Doctrine*, xxxiii. See Higton, "Reconstructing," 3.

6. Lindbeck, *The Nature of Doctrine*, xxxiii.

7. Lindbeck, *The Nature of Doctrine*, xxxiv.

8. Lindbeck, *The Nature of Doctrine*, xxxiv; cf. xxix.

9. This had been the focus of Lindbeck's work for decades. See Granfield, "George Lindbeck," 152. Within this 1967 interview,

Due to Lindbeck's intention to make the volume tenable for nontheological and theological study of doctrine and religion, *The Nature of Doctrine* is a complicated read. Lindbeck later lamented that most reviewers missed his ecumenical focus. In the "Forward to the German Edition of *The Nature of Doctrine*," originally published in 1994, Lindbeck says, "This is not the book it was ten years ago when it was first published. It was captured by unanticipated interest groups who so shaped the public reception that even I, the author, now read it partly through their eyes."[10] He argues that this happened because his "intended audience had largely vanished."[11] The ecumenical movement shifted its focus away from doctrinal reconciliation and toward Justice, Peace and the Integrity of Creation (JPIC). Various readers instead saw *The Nature of Doctrine* as a contribution to the ongoing conversation, with participants like Stanley Hauerwas and Alasdair MacIntyre, about the ways in which modernism has been replaced by "a new culture, religious, and theological situation."[12] Lindbeck argues that if he had initially intended to write a volume like that, *The Nature of Doctrine* would have been a very different book. Given Lindbeck's initial intentions for *The Nature of Doctrine*, I will, in this chapter, emphasize the ecumenical aspects of the book. I will, however, also

---

Lindbeck refers to his interest in "comparative dogmatics or symbolics," or what German scholars call *Konfessionskunde*, which he says is "a comparative study of the major theological dogmatic traditions in Christendom." He says that he anticipates a course in comparative dogmatics as his "continuing major lecture course from now on."

10. Lindbeck, *The Nature of Doctrine*, xxix.
11. Lindbeck, *The Nature of Doctrine*, xxix.
12. Lindbeck, *The Nature of Doctrine*, xxxi.

look at the broader implications of the book, in dialogue with Lindbeck's larger project, for theological practice.

DOCTRINAL RECONCILIATION WITHOUT CAPITULATION

Lindbeck begins the first chapter saying, "Over and over again in recent years, there have been reports from Roman Catholic, Orthodox, and Protestant theologians engaged in dialogues sponsored by their respective churches that they are in basic agreement on such topics as the Eucharist, ministry, justification, or even the papacy, and yet they continue—so they claim—to adhere to their historic and once-divisive convictions."[13] These ecumenists came to see, through study and dialogue, that positions they once saw as contradictory are actually reconcilable. These ecumenical statements, however, are often treated with skepticism. How can, for example, Lutherans and Catholics come to have a shared statement on justification while neither group has revised their doctrine?

To make sense of this confusion surrounding doctrinal reconciliation without capitulation, Lindbeck proposes a typology for understanding religion and religious doctrine. Lindbeck calls the first type "cognitive-propositional." This approach "emphasizes the cognitive aspects of religion and stresses the ways in which church doctrines function as informative propositions or truth claims about objective realities."[14] He associates this type with both traditional orthodoxies and analytic approaches to religion. Lindbeck calls the second type "experiential-expressivist." This approach "interprets doctrines as noninformative

13. Lindbeck, *The Nature of Doctrine*, 1.
14. Lindbeck, *The Nature of Doctrine*, 2.

Postliberal

and nondiscursive symbols of inner feelings, attitudes, or existential orientations,"[15] and it also assumes that there is a "core experience" that is "said to be common to a wide diversity of religions."[16] This understanding can be traced to the liberal theological tradition that flows from Friedrich Schleiermacher. Lindbeck argues that the third type is a hybrid, two-dimensional approach that combines the first two types. Lindbeck associates this type with Catholic theologians Karl Rahner and Bernard Lonergan.[17]

Lindbeck argues that within these first three types, the possibility of doctrinal reconciliation without capitulation is impossible. Within the first two types, "either doctrinal reconciliation or constancy must be rejected."[18] For the first type, "if a doctrine is once true, it is always true, and if it is once false, it is always false."[19] So, there is no possibility of reconciling, for example, historic affirmations and rejections of transubstantiation. For a propositionalist, the only way ecumenical agreement can be reached is if "one or both sides abandon their earlier positions."[20]

For the second type, because doctrines function as nondiscursive symbols, their meaning is polyvalent. Therefore, two people could hold to the same doctrine, such as transubstantiation, while meaning very different things by it, or they could claim to hold to a "new" doctrine while meaning much the same thing. Lindbeck argues that within this approach, "[Doctrines] are not crucial for harmony or conflict in underlying feelings, attitudes,

---

15. Lindbeck, *The Nature of Doctrine*, 2.
16. Lindbeck, *The Nature of Doctrine*, 18.
17. Lindbeck, *The Nature of Doctrine*, 2, 17–18.
18. Lindbeck, *The Nature of Doctrine*, 2.
19. Lindbeck, *The Nature of Doctrine*, 2.
20. Lindbeck, *The Nature of Doctrine*, 2.

existential orientations, or practices, rather than by what happens on the level of symbolic (including doctrinal) objectifications."[21] This approach can go so far as to affirm that a Buddhist and Christian can more or less have the same faith even though they have different symbolic systems.

Lindbeck argues that the third type has advantages over both of the first two types, but still falls short because of how difficult it is to simply combine the cognitive-propositional and experiential-expressivist types. This approach does not necessarily exclude the possibility of doctrinal reconciliation without capitulation, but it has difficulty in determining the criteria by which one can discern when a doctrinal development is consistent with the official teaching of the church. He argues, "Even at their best, as in Rahner and Lonergan, they resort to complicated gymnastics and to that extent are unpersuasive."[22]

Due to the difficulties in these first three types, Lindbeck proposes a fourth type—the "cultural-linguistic" approach. This perspective says that "religions resemble languages together with their correlative forms of life and are thus similar to cultures."[23] Moreover, "a religion can be viewed as a kind of cultural and/or linguistic framework or medium that shapes the entirety of life and thought."[24] This approach is not anti-cognitive or anti-experiential, but it avoids a one-dimensional approach to religion and does not simply seek to combine the cognitive and the experiential. Instead, the cultural-linguistic approach sublates the cognitive and experiential, including both beliefs and

21. Lindbeck, *The Nature of Doctrine*, 3.
22. Lindbeck, *The Nature of Doctrine*, 3.
23. Lindbeck, *The Nature of Doctrine*, 4.
24. Lindbeck, *The Nature of Doctrine*, 19; see 66–67.

symbols.²⁵ He says, "it is similar to an idiom that makes possible the description of realities, the formulation of beliefs, and the experiencing of inner attitudes, feelings, and sentiments."²⁶ While experiential-expressive views of religion seek to find a common core of all religious experience, within the cultural-linguistic approach,

> Adherents of different religions do not diversely thematize the same experience; rather they have different experiences. Buddhist compassion, Christian love and—if I may cite a quasi-religious phenomenon—French revolutionary *fraternité* are not diverse modifications of a single fundamental human awareness, emotion, attitude, or sentiment, but are radically (i.e., from the root) distinct ways of experiencing and being oriented toward self, neighbor, and cosmos.²⁷

Within this type, doctrines function as "communally authoritative rules of discourse, attitude, and action,"²⁸ or "communally authoritative teachings regarding beliefs and practices that are considered essential to the identity or welfare of the group in question."²⁹ Lindbeck clarifies his definition further with four points, with particular attention to how doctrines function in the church. First, doctrines are unavoidable. Every Christian group, even those who claim to be creedless, have doctrines. Second, he says that doctrines can be "formally stated or informally operative, but in any case they indicate what constitutes

25. Lindbeck, *The Nature of Doctrine*, 20–22. See Michener, *Postliberal*, 67.

26. Lindbeck, *The Nature of Doctrine*, 19; see 33–34.

27. Lindbeck, *The Nature of Doctrine*, 26.

28. Lindbeck, *The Nature of Doctrine*, 4.

29. Lindbeck, *The Nature of Doctrine*, 60.

faithful adherence to a community."[30] So, for some groups, such as biblicistic Protestants, trinitarian doctrine may be operative even though there is no official endorsement of the Nicene Creed, while for some liberal Protestants, the Nicene Creed may remain official, but not be operative. Third, "controversy is the normal means whereby implicit doctrines become explicit, and operational ones official."[31] Official doctrines, like the Christological and trinitarian doctrines of the early Christian creeds, arose in the midst of controversy or conflict.[32] Fourth, Lindbeck distinguishes between theology and doctrine. He does so by noting that there can be theological diversity within a community that has doctrinal agreement: "Those who agree on explicitly formulated doctrines may disagree sharply on how to interpret, justify, or defined them."[33] So, for example, Roman Catholics may doctrinally agree on transubstantiation, but different Catholics may have different interpretations of transubstantiation and defend the doctrine in different ways.

Lindbeck argues that a regulative approach better allows for doctrinal reconciliation without capitulation. He says, "Rules, unlike propositions or expressive symbols, retain an invariant meaning under changing conditions of compatibility and conflict."[34] A regulative approach is preferable to a merely propositional approach because it allows for the "permanence of doctrine amid historical

30. Lindbeck, *The Nature of Doctrine*, 60.

31. Lindbeck, *The Nature of Doctrine*, 61. Lindeck notes that there are exceptions, such as the Marian dogmas recognized by the Roman Catholic Church in the nineteenth and twentieth centuries. See 61, 82–84.

32. Lindbeck, *The Nature of Doctrine*, 61–62, 80–81.

33. Lindbeck, *The Nature of Doctrine*, 62, 78.

34. Lindbeck, *The Nature of Doctrine*, 4.

change" and closely connects doctrines to church praxis.[35] As an example, Lindbeck points to the rules "drive on the left" and "drive on the right." He notes that these rules are "unequivocal in meaning and unequivocally opposed, yet both may be binding: one in Britain and the other in the United States."[36] Neither of the rules must change to accommodate the other. Instead, people must understand when each rule applies.

Doctrines thus function like a grammar, providing guidance for proper Christian speech.[37] Lindbeck argues that this regulative understanding of doctrine is not new, but goes back to the early Christian *regula fidei*.[38] His view recognizes that while certain grammatical rules may be inadequate in a certain sense, they are also indispensable, especially for those who are beginners.[39] To become religious is to become fluent within a religion's language—to "interiorize a set of skills by practice and training."[40] Thus, to become a fluent Christian "involves learning the story of Israel and of Jesus well enough to interpret and experience oneself and one's world in its terms."[41]

TOWARD A POSTLIBERAL THEOLOGY

The final chapter of *The Nature of Doctrine*, "Toward a Postliberal Theology," serves as "an addendum to the main

---

35. Lindbeck, *The Nature of Doctrine*, 77.
36. Lindbeck, *The Nature of Doctrine*, 4.
37. Lindbeck, *The Nature of Doctrine*, 67–68.
38. Lindbeck, *The Nature of Doctrine*, 4, 80.
39. Lindbeck, *The Nature of Doctrine*, 68, 81–82.
40. Lindbeck, *The Nature of Doctrine*, 21.
41. Lindbeck, *The Nature of Doctrine*, 20.

argument of the book, but a necessary one."[42] Herein, he discusses the implications of his postliberal, cultural-linguistic understanding of religion for the practice of theology. In particular, he focuses on faithfulness, applicability, and intelligibility. Lindbeck argues that in the history of Christian theology in the West, faithfulness has generally been associated with systematic/dogmatic theology, applicability with pastoral theology, and intelligibility with foundational/apologetic theology, though each theological subdiscipline includes each of these emphases.

Faithfulness and Intratextuality

Lindbeck argues, "The task of descriptive (dogmatic or systematic) theology is to give a normative explication of the meaning a religion has for its adherents."[43] He contends that an approach to dogmatic theology that is consistent with a cultural-linguistic approach to religion is an "intratextual" one. An "extratextual" approach locates meaning outside of the text or semiotic system of a religion in either objective realities or common human experiences, whereas for an intratextual approach, "the meaning is immanent. Meaning is constituted by the uses of a specific language rather than being distinguishable from it."[44] As an example of this, Lindbeck argues that one comes to understand the meaning of the word "God," or a gesture like the sign of the cross, by examining its role within a religious tradition and how it shapes the lives of its adherents. Within an intratextual method,

---

42. Lindbeck, *The Nature of Doctrine*, 98.
43. Lindbeck, *The Nature of Doctrine*, 99.
44. Lindbeck, *The Nature of Doctrine*, 100.

Postliberal

one can describe Christianity internally, but one can also understand and interpret everything by and within Christianity, just as one can describe all of reality in French or English.[45] Lindbeck develops this intratextual method in dialogue with a variety of sources, but two of them are of central importance—the cultural anthropology of Clifford Geertz (1926–2006) and the hermeneutical work of his Yale colleague Hans Frei (1922–1988).

Geertz and Theology as Ethnography

Geertz has a semiotic understanding of culture. He sees humanity as "an animal suspended in webs of significance he himself has spun" and culture as those webs. The practice of studying culture is not as "an experimental science in search of law," but rather as "an interpretive one in search of meaning."[46] Anthropologists make these interpretive moves through the practice of ethnography, which Geertz insists is not simply the application of a method or a technique. Rather, Geertz says that ethnography is, to borrow a term from Gilbert Ryle (1900–1976), "thick description."[47]

Geertz also borrows an example of thick description from Ryle. Imagine two boys contracting their right eyelids. In the first boy, it is an involuntary twitch, while in the second boy, the contracting of the eyelid is a signal to communicate something to a friend. Geertz notes that as movements, both are identical, yet the difference between the twitch of the first boy and the wink of the other is vast, for the winker is not simply making a bodily movement,

---

45. Lindbeck, *The Nature of Doctrine*, 100–101.
46. Geertz, *The Interpretation*, 5.
47. Geertz, *The Interpretation*, 6.

but is seeking to communicate in a particular way. Geertz says he is doing so "(1) deliberately, (2) to someone in particular, (3) to impart a particular message, (4) according to a socially established code, and (5) without cognizance of the rest of the company."[48] The issue can be even more complicated, for suppose there is also a third boy that parodies the first boy in order to mock him. Or suppose this third boy winks to make others in the room think that he and another person have some type of social agreement when they in fact do not have one. Geertz argues that when an anthropologist practices ethnography, what they are doing is not "thin description"—simply describing a boy contracting his eyelid, but rather the work of "thick description." They seek to interpret what he is actually doing, namely, communicating something to another person based upon a previous agreement or understood social convention, like mocking another person's convulsions.[49] So according to Geertz, "Doing ethnography is like trying to read a manuscript—foreign, faded, full of ellipses, incoherencies, suspicious emendations, and tendentious commentaries, but written not in conventionalized graphs of sound but in transient examples of shaped behavior."[50]

Therefore, for Geertz, culture, "this acted document," is public, and it is so because meaning is public. To participate within a culture, and to communicate within it and interpret within it,[51] one must have a variety of "habits, skills, knowledge and talents."[52] Ethnographers must at-

48. Geertz, *The Interpretation*, 6.

49. Geertz, *The Interpretation*, 7.

50. Geertz, *The Interpretation*, 10.

51. Geertz says, "Anthropologists don't study villages . . .; they study in villages" (Geertz, *The Interpretation*, 22).

52. Geertz, *The Interpretation*, 12.

tend to the behavior of people and come to an understanding of behaviors and "the role they play . . . in an ongoing pattern of life."[53]

Geertz does not attempt to provide a universal theory of cultural interpretation. Ethnographers should not attempt to "codify abstract regularities," but instead "to make thick description possible, not to generalize across cases but to generalize within them."[54] This stems from Geertz's critique of the "uniformitarian view of man"—the view that argues there is "the image of a constant human nature independent of time, place, and circumstances."[55]

Such critiques of a universalized human also extend to Geertz's understanding of religion. According to Geertz, one cannot define religion generally as "[humanity's] most fundamental orientation to reality," or to a belief in the afterlife or providence, or other similar definitions.[56] There are too many differences between polytheistic Hindus and monotheistic Sunni Muslims, between Confucians and Calvinists, or even between Zen and Tibetan Buddhists, to give religion a general definition. To provide one would be to derive what A. L. Kroeber calls a "fake universal."[57] Geertz instead studies religion as a cultural system.

Lindbeck argues that the work of theology is like the work of an ethnographer. One cannot simply

53. Geertz, *The Interpretation*, 17.

54. Geertz, *The Interpretation*, 26.

55. Geertz, *The Interpretation*, 35. He says further, "Whatever else modern anthropology asserts—and it seems to have asserted almost everything at one time or another—it is firm in the conviction that men unmodified by the customs of particular places do not in fact exist, have never existed, and most important, could not in the very nature of the case exist" (35).

56. Geertz, *The Interpretation*, 40.

57. Geertz, *The Interpretation*, 40.

isolate various features of a religious tradition and from them characterize the entire tradition. One must have a familiarity with a semiotic system in order to understand the various signs within it. Lindbeck says, "[Religions] all have relatively fixed canons of writings that they treat as exemplary or normative instantiations of their semiotic codes. One test of faithfulness for all of them is the degree to which descriptions correspond to the semiotic universe paradigmatically encoded in holy writ."[58]

Frei and Figural Reading of Scripture

In the case of Christianity, this collection of holy writ is canonized in the Bible, made up of the Old and New Testaments. Lindbeck argues that to describe the basic meaning of the Bible is an intratextual task—one in which one comes to understand the world in light of God's engagement with Israel, Jesus, and the church. He says, "A scriptural world is . . . able to absorb the universe. It supplies the interpretive framework within which believers seek to live their lives and understand reality."[59] Lindbeck argues that this happens apart from a formal theory of how it happens. Augustine, for example, did not discuss the relation of Scripture to reality in these terms, but, Lindbeck argues that one could interpret his entire project as the attempt "to insert everything from Platonism and the Pelagian problem to the fall of Rome into the world of the Bible."[60] Later figures, like Thomas Aquinas and even Schleiermacher, sought to do the same with Aristotelianism and German idealism

58. Lindbeck, *The Nature of Doctrine*, 102.

59. Lindbeck, *The Nature of Doctrine*, 103. For clarification on what Lindbeck means by arguing the text absorbs the world, see Marshall, "Absorbing the World."

60. Lindbeck, *The Nature of Doctrine*, 103.

in their own days. He says, "The way they described extrascriptural realities and experience, so it can be argued, was shaped by biblical categories much more than was warranted by their formal methodologies."[61]

Within this understanding, there is an emphasis upon typological or figural devices, which are used first to understand the unity of the canon, and second to understand reality. He argues, "Typology was used to incorporate the Hebrew Scriptures into a canon that focused on Christ, and then, by extension, to embrace extrabiblical reality."[62] This largely continued in the Reformers, who emphasized Scripture's self-interpreting character (*scriptura sui ipsius interpres*).[63]

Lindbeck says, "Unlike allegorizing, typological interpretation did not empty Old Testament or postbiblical personages and events of their own reality, and therefore they constituted a powerful means for imaginatively incorporating all being into a Christ-centered world."[64] Lindbeck insists that an intratextual approach does not use Scripture as a metaphor for common human experience. The cross, for example, is not simply a representation of human suffering. Instead, "suffering should be cruciform."[65] Intratextual theology describes the world in scriptural terms, rather than trying to translate scriptural categories into a modern framework.

Lindbeck argues that the work of his colleague, Hans Frei, has significantly influenced his understanding of

---

61. Lindbeck, *The Nature of Doctrine*, 103; see 109.
62. Lindbeck, *The Nature of Doctrine*, 103.
63. Lindbeck, *The Nature of Doctrine*, 104.
64. Lindbeck, *The Nature of Doctrine*, 103–04.
65. Lindbeck, *The Nature of Doctrine*, 104.

biblical hermeneutics.[66] In *The Eclipse of Biblical Narrative*, Frei explains, "Western Christian reading of the Bible in the days before the rise of historical criticism in the eighteenth century was usually strongly realistic, i.e. at once literal and historical, and not only doctrinal or edifying."[67] Premodern approaches permitted other approaches to reading Scripture, such as allegorical or typological ones, but they could not violate the literal sense of the text. Frei says, "Long before a minor modern school of thought made the biblical 'history of salvation' a special and historical sequence for historiographical and theological inquiry, Christian preachers and theological commentators, Augustine the most notable among them, had envisioned the real world as formed by the sequence told by the biblical stories."[68] This way of reading Scripture persisted through the Renaissance and the Reformation.

Frei identifies three key elements in this classical way of reading Scripture. First, readers assumed that the biblical story "referred to and described actual historical occurrences."[69] Second, the various biblical stories fit together into one narrative, and earlier persons or events

---

66. E.g., Lindbeck, "The Church," 202n9. John Wright has also argued that various Roman Catholic theologians associated with the *nouvelle théologie*, like Henri de Lubac and Yves Congar, influenced the "first-generation postliberals." See Wright, "The Silent Shifting," 13–30.

67. Frei, *Eclipse*, 1. Frei elsewhere also uses the term "history-like" to refer to the narratives in Scripture.

68. Frei, *Eclipse*, 1. While Frei discusses narrative here, it is important to note that Frei sought to distance himself from what later came to be known as "narrative theology." He also resisted an attempt to develop or to uncritically draw upon a general hermeneutic or a general theory of narrative. See Frei, "Literal Reading," 59; Lindbeck, "Scripture," 82n3; Higton, "Forward," xi.

69. Frei, *Eclipse*, 2.

Postliberal

often functioned as figures or types within later stories. Third, "since the world truly rendered by combining biblical narratives into one was indeed the one and only real world, it must in principle embrace the experience of any present age and reader."[70]

Throughout much of the volume, Frei traces the shift away from classical, figural exegesis. He says it was was due not only to the rise of historical criticism but also to Deism, rationalism, romanticism, pietism, fundamentalism, and other cultural and theological developments. Frei says that because of such developments, "There is now a logical distinction and reflective distance between the stories and the 'reality' they depict."[71] There came to be a separation between the biblical world and the real world, between the literal and historical sense. These exegetes, of various theological persuasions, came to believe that "whether or not the story is true history, its *meaning* is detachable from the story that sets it forth."[72] This undermined the possibility of figural exegesis. Lindbeck says that because of these shifts, "Scripture ceased to function as the lens through which theologians viewed the world and instead became primarily an object of study whose religiously significant or literal meaning was located outside itself."[73]

Lindbeck argues that while not every passage in Scripture is a narrative the overarching narrative of Scripture, which climaxes in the ministry of Jesus Christ, holds the various writings—the laws, poems, prophesies, apocalypses, and letters (among other genres)—together into a coherent canon. Lindbeck points to David Kelsey's

70. Frei, *Eclipse*, 3.
71. Frei, *Eclipse*, 5.
72. Frei, *Eclipse*, 6.
73. Lindbeck, *The Nature of Doctrine*, 105.

words that "Barth took scripture to be one vast, loosely-structured, non-fiction novel."[74] And the primary purpose of Scripture is—again to quote Kelsey—"to render a character" or "to offer an identity description of an agent," the God of Abraham, Isaac, Jacob, and Jesus.[75] It does not primarily tell us who God is in God's essence, but rather provides accounts of God's works and interactions with creation in different times and places.

Within this project, Lindbeck does not seek to repristinate precritical exegesis, and he also does not want to deny the gains of modern biblical criticism.[76] He instead seeks to develop a postliberal or postcritical way of reading Scripture that can recognize the distinction between Frei's realistic narratives and modern, historical, or scientific descriptions or reconstructions of historical events. He says, "The Bible is often 'history-like' even when it is not 'likely history.' It can therefore be taken seriously in the first respect as a delineator of the character of divine and human agents, even when its history or science is challenged."[77] He notes that the parables of Jesus demonstrate this. No one assumes that the various parables of Jesus report historical narratives, but they do, nevertheless, communicate something about the character of God.

74. Kelsey, *Proving Doctrine*, 48.

75. Kelsey, *Proving Doctrine*, 48.

76. Lindbeck argues that "historical criticism influences the theological-literary interpretation of texts" (108). He points, for example, at the work of Gerhard von Rad, who offers a postcritical reading of the Old Testament that differs in many ways from the work of precritical exegetes. See also Phillips and Ockholm, "A Panel Discussion," 247.

77. Lindbeck, *The Nature of Doctrine*, 108.

Applicability and the Future

Lindbeck connects applicability with futurology, which does not primarily deal with predicting the future, but instead with the attempt to "shape present action to fit the anticipated and hoped-for future."[78] He notes that this concern has often been associated with biblical prophets, who "proclaim what is both faithful and applicable in a given situation, and they oppose proposals that, whatever their apparent practicality, are doomed because of their unfaithfulness to God's future."[79] The purpose of a Christian futurology is to discern how the church should act as it hopefully anticipates God's coming kingdom. A postliberal approach to this futurology seeks to do this intratextually.

While Lindbeck notes that various current cultural trends make a widespread embrace of a postliberal, intratextual approach unlikely, one cannot proceed on the basis of current trends alone. He says that while it may seem counterintuitive, the world may, in the future, be dependent upon "communal enclaves that socialize their members into highly particular outlooks supportive of concern for others rather than for individual rights and entitlements, and a sense of responsibility for the wider society rather than for personal fulfillment."[80] They may be more relevant by focusing upon their own "intratextual outlooks and forms of life,"[81] by focusing on how they can be faithful. On this basis, Lindbeck argues that postliberal

78. Lindbeck, *The Nature of Doctrine*, 111.

79. Lindbeck, *The Nature of Doctrine*, 111.

80. Lindbeck, *The Nature of Doctrine*, 113. This is not the first time Lindbeck has made such a proposal. See Lindbeck, "The Sectarian Future."

81. Lindbeck, *The Nature of Doctrine*, 114.

theologies may very well be more applicable than accommodationist, liberal ones in the future.

Intelligibility and Apologetics

Lindbeck here acknowledges that some may see his account of intratextuality as both relativistic and fideistic. Many, both conservative and liberal, propositional and expressivist, may argue that what is needed is an apologetic approach or a neutral foundation from which one can evaluate the various religions. Apart from this foundation, does not the choice of a religious tradition seem arbitrary? Lindbeck explains,

> Postliberals are bound to be skeptical, not about missions, but about apologetics and foundations. To the degree that religions are like languages and cultures, they can no more be taught by means of translation than can Chinese or French. What is said in one idiom can to some extent be conveyed in a foreign tongue, but no one learns to understand and speak Chinese by simply hearing and reading translations. Resistance to translation does not wholly exclude apologetics, but this must be of an ad hoc and nonfoundational variety rather than standing at the center of theology. The grammar of religion, like that of language, cannot be explicated or learned by analysis of experience, but only by practice . . . In short, religions, like languages, can be understood only in their own terms, not by transposing them into an alien speech.[82]

82. Lindbeck, *The Nature of Doctrine*, 115. Frei refers to *ad hoc* apologetics in *Types*, 161. Lindbeck later says in response to a question from Alister McGrath, "[T]here is no single logic of coming [to faith]. There is a logic of belief. There is a structure of Christian faith. But the ways in which God calls us through the Holy Spirit to come to

Postliberal

Lindbeck argues, however, that this does not lead to a ghettoizing of theology as a discipline. Rather, it can provide theologians with the freedom to engage closely with other disciplines, from philosophy to the social and natural sciences. For Lindbeck, antifoundationalism must not be equated with irrationalism.[83] Different fields of inquiry have different standards of rationality.

A particular religion cannot be wholly disproved from the outset. Rather, one can test a religion analogously to how one tests a scientific theory, through confirmation or disconfirmation on the basis of how successfully a religion makes sense of available data. One can thus judge the reasonableness of a religion on its ability to assimilate, to "provide an intelligible interpretation in its own terms of the varied situations and realities adherents encounter."[84] This does not mean that a person can decide upon what religious tradition to follow on the basis of reason alone, but it can allow her to take reason into account.

Lindbeck argues that his views on the relation of faith and reason are consistent with those of various premodern Christian theologians. Though Martin Luther attacked "whore reason," Lindbeck argues that Luther was not a fideist. Luther drew upon reason in his teaching, both positively and in opposition to other Christians and pagans. Lindbeck also argues that Thomas Aquinas'

---

believe are so varied that you cannot possibly make generalizations. I would add: people are inevitably committed to working within a given conceptual language system. We Christians think, look and argue from within the faith. There's no getting outside the faith to objectively compare different options. Why follow Christ rather than someone else? I find myself thinking very much along the epistemological lines of Alasdair MacIntyre." Phillips and Ockholm, "A Panel Discussion," 252.

83. Lindbeck, *The Nature of Doctrine*, 116.

84. Lindbeck, *The Nature of Doctrine*, 117.

use of reason "does not lead to foundational or natural theology of the modern type."[85] As noted previously, his five ways are not attempts at demonstrative proofs for the existence of God, but probabilistic arguments. Lindbeck concludes, "Both of these thinkers, despite their material differences, can be viewed as holding that revelation dominates all aspects of the theological enterprise, but without excluding a subsidiary use of philosophical and experiential considerations in the explication and defense of the faith."[86]

Given this approach to the relation between faith and reason, how does one preach the gospel in the contemporary, postchristian world? Lindbeck argues that the method most consistent with his postliberal approach more closely resembles the early Christian practice of catechesis, which has been the dominant approach to passing on the faith throughout the church's history:

> Pagan converts to the catholic mainstream did not, for the most part, first understand the faith and then decide to become Christians; rather, the process was reversed: they first decided and then they understood. More precisely, they were first attracted by the Christian community and form of life. The reasons for attraction ranged from the noble to the ignoble and were as diverse as the individuals involved; but for whatever motives, they submitted themselves to prolonged catechetical instruction in which they practiced new modes of behavior and learned the stories of Israel and their fulfillment in Christ. Only after they had acquired proficiency in the alien Christian language and form of life were they

---

85. Lindbeck, *The Nature of Doctrine*, 117.
86. Lindbeck, *The Nature of Doctrine*, 117.

> deemed able intelligently and responsibly to profess the faith, to be baptized.[87]

While this model of catechesis in the second and third centuries ceased after Christianity became the dominant religion of the Roman empire, Lindbeck argues that the practice of catechesis continued "in diluted form."[88] Lindbeck recognizes that recapturing this practice of catechesis in the current context is next to impossible, but posits that perhaps as "dechristianization reduces Christians to a small minority, they will need for the sake of survival to form communities that strive without traditionalist rigidity to cultivate their native tongue and learn to act accordingly."[89]

Lindbeck thus concludes *The Nature of Doctrine* by arguing that while a postliberal theology is capable of being faithful, applicable, and intelligible, that it is not likely to be pursued in a widespread way. He holds out hope, however, because of the work of some younger theologians who are going about the work of "absorbing the universe into the biblical world." He prays, "May their tribe increase."[90]

CONCLUSION

There has been much confusion about the term "postliberal[ism]" and how it should be defined. In a panel discussion at the 1995 Wheaton College Theology Conference, which sought to bring postliberals and evangelicals

---

87. Lindbeck, *The Nature of Doctrine*, 118. Lindbeck's perspective here comes not only from his study of history, but from his experience as the child of missionaries in China. Phillips and Ockholm, "A Panel Discussion," 251.

88. Lindbeck, *The Nature of Doctrine*, 118.

89. Lindbeck, *The Nature of Doctrine*, 119–20.

90. Lindbeck, *The Nature of Doctrine*, 121.

into conversation, Lindbeck argues that while he did not initially intend to define it this way, first and foremost, postliberalism is a "research program" or "an attempt to recover premodern scriptural interpretation in contemporary form."[91] He then clarifies what he means in this context by the term premodern. First, it refers to the time before modern foundationalism and the various controversies and debates about biblical inspiration or inerrancy. He contends that "postliberalism is agnostic about these controversies and positions that came out of them, just as premodern scriptural interpretation was."[92] Second, he uses the term premodern here to refer to the time before the rise of modern individualism, which in various traditions that emphasized "conversionist revivalism" modified or rejected classical ways of reading Scripture. He concludes, "To speak of individualism in this context means that postliberalism tries to divorce itself from the antiecclesial, the anti- or low-sacramentalism and anti- or noncreedal ways of reading Scripture that have prevailed on the modern evangelical side."[93]

91. Phillips and Ockholm, "A Panel Discussion," 246. They thus differ from evangelicals who are "members of communities, institutions, movements that are historically associated with inerrancy controversies on the one hand and conversionist revivalism on the other." Lindbeck identifies Hans Frei as the most significant figure in this program.

92. Phillips and Ockholm, "A Panel Discussion," 246. He also repeats his claim from *The Nature of Doctrine* that he does not want to negate the gains of biblical criticism, but he does want to place it "in a very subordinate role as far as the theologically significant reading of Scripture is concerned" (247).

93. Phillips and Ockholm, "A Panel Discussion," 246. Lindbeck notes that this actually means there is some overlap between the theological concerns of some postliberals and some of the evangelical participants in the dialogue, like Alister McGrath, who emphasize the need to renew evangelicalism by "recovering heritage" (247).

Postliberal

Some of the participants in the conference critiqued the "lack of substantive theological work on the postliberal side," but Lindbeck argues that this is a misplaced criticism. He says, "It's misplaced because the research program is one regarding methods of reading Scripture, not specifically regarding the development of any single theological outlook. If I do theology (and I have done a fair amount of substantive theology), it's Lutheran theology in the Lutheran confessional tradition. For George Hunsinger it's in the Reformed confessional tradition."[94] In the next chapter, I will turn to Lindbeck's later ecclesiological work, demonstrating that he was not a person fixated on issues of theological method, but a theologian concerned about the unity of the churches.

Discussion Questions

1. Lindbeck argues that a "theory of religion and doctrine cannot be ecumenically useful unless it is nonecumenically possible." Is this true?
2. What types of doctrine does Lindbeck identify?
3. What are doctrines? How do doctrines function within communities?
4. What is the difference between thin and thick description? How could we practice thick description in theology?
5. What would it look to interpret Scripture intratextually?
6. What does it mean for apologetics to be ad hoc?

---

94. Phillips and Ockholm, "A Panel Discussion," 247.

7. What are the implications of Lindbeck's understanding of theology for preaching and teaching?

7

ISRAELOLOGIST

Given the attention *The Nature of Doctrine* received, one might have expected Lindbeck to spend the rest of his career clarifying its ideas and defending the book from its critics. Instead, Bruce Marshall says, his work was devoted "mainly to the elaboration of ideas that were at most latent in *The Nature of Doctrine*."[1] Lindbeck focused on issues like the recovery of classical ways of reading Scripture[2] and above all to ecclesiological issues, in particular, the relation of the church to Israel. Marshall notes that this shift in his thought also had "deep roots in his own theological history."[3] Principally, he continues to maintain his emphasis upon *Konfessionskunde*, or "comparative dogmatics," but with a different focus. He says in the "Foreword to the German Edition of *The Nature of Doctrine*," originally published in 1994,

---

1. Marshall, "Introduction," xi–xii.
2. E.g., Lindbeck, "Scripture."
3. Marshall, "Introduction," xii.

> As far as my own work is concerned, it has become clear to me in the last decade, not least because of the discussions prompted by this book, that a comparative dogmatics needs to take a different form than I originally envisioned. It should start with ecclesiology and, included in that, with what might be called "Israel-ology." The two cannot be separated in a scriptural narrative approach: Israel and the Church are one elect people, and rethinking their relation is fundamental to ecumenism. This thinking must be theological, i.e. based on Scripture as it functions in communities for which the scriptural witness to the God of Israel and of Jesus is authoritative. It makes use of analyses such as are found in the present work, but is not based on them.[4]

His emphasis upon the relation of the church to Israel did not come out of nowhere, but actually went back to his work in the 1960s. While he was an observer at the Second Vatican Council, he argued that one should understand the church and Israel "in parallel."[5] In the late 1980s, he began referring to the church as "Israel-like." While he continued to use this language to a certain extent in his later writings, within a few years he begins to refer to the church "as Israel," for as he says in a 2006 interview, "'Seeing the church as Israel' is better because it suggests that there is a sense in which it really is Israel and not merely similar."[6] In this work, Lindbeck resists the tendency within the ecumenical movement to bracket the question of the relation of individual churches to the one, holy, catholic, and apostolic

---

4. Lindbeck, "Foreword," xxxii.

5. See Lindbeck, "A Protestant View." During that time, he also published two brief pieces on Jewish-Christian dialogue. See "The Jews" and "Jewish-Christian."

6. Lindbeck, "Performing the Faith," 29.

church, and instead argues, "Ecclesiology and ecumenism are inseparable."[7] And beyond this claim, he argues that "the search for unity goes awry apart from a sense of the church as Israel."[8]

THE CHURCH AS ISRAEL

In his 1990 "How My Mind Has Changed" article in *Christian Century*, Lindbeck argues, "Renewal depends, I have come to think, on the spread of the proficiency in premodern yet postcritical Bible reading, on restricting the churches into something like pre-Constantinian organization patterns, and on the development of an Israel-like understanding of the church."[9] Lindbeck sees these three elements as interrelated, which he demonstrates in his definition of the church as "the messianic pilgrim people of God typologically shaped by Israel's story."[10] In this, Lindbeck does not deny the creedal marks of the church (one, holy, catholic, and apostolic) or the Reformation emphasis upon the church as *creatura verbi*—a creature of the word—but develops them further by describing the church "as Israel."[11]

Lindbeck argues that the definition of the church as "messianic pilgrim people of God" has the most ecumenical potential, for it is amenable to both Protestants

---

7. Lindbeck, "The Church as Israel," 78.

8. Lindbeck, "The Church as Israel," 80. For more in depth treatments of Lindbeck's Israelology, see Brown, *George Lindbeck*; Ochs, *Another Reformation*, ch. 2.

9. Lindbeck, "Confession and Community," 495.

10. Lindbeck, "The Church," 179. Lindbeck repeats much of the same material in "The Story-Shaped Church."

11. Lindbeck, "The Church," 179; Lindbeck, "The Church as Israel."

and Roman Catholics. It was first treated as a central motif in H. F. Hamilton's (1876–1919) *The People of God: An Inquiry Into Christian Origins*.[12] Later Protestant interpreters, like Lesslie Newbigin (1909–1998), treated the church as people of God alongside the church as body of Christ, community of the Holy Spirit, and other descriptors.[13] In the Second Vatican Council's Dogmatic Constitution of the Church, *Lumen Gentium*, the church is treated as the people of God alongside sacrament of unity and institution.

He notes, however, that an emphasis upon the church as people of God only has ecumenical potential if it has biblical warrant, for "Without this, it can be neither catholic nor ecumenical."[14] Lindbeck does not deny that there are times when the church has needed to utilize nonbiblical language in order to remain faithful to the gospel and/or intelligible in the face of new situations, such as in the case of the christological and trinitarian formulations of the ancient creeds or in opposition to the institution of slavery. He acknowledges that this may also be true in certain cases in ecclesiology, but these examples are the exception and not the rule. He says, "The burden of proof is on those whose fundamental categories for thinking about the church are nonbiblical."[15] Others may argue that some other designation, like "body of Christ," is more fundamental, but Lindbeck decides to "proceed on the doctrinally and ecumenically mandated hypothesis that

---

12. Published by Oxford University Press in 1912.
13. See Newbigin, *Household of God*.
14. Lindbeck, "The Church," 181.
15. Lindbeck, "The Church," 182.

Israelologist

the church was primarily the people of God in the biblical writings, and ask what that meant."[16]

Lindbeck claims that this approach has strong support. Early Christians were a Jewish sect that followed a crucified and risen Messiah. While they came to welcome uncircumcised Gentiles, they still sought to maintain their Jewish identity, and their communal self-understanding came from the Hebrew Scriptures—the Tanakh (or for Grecian Jews, the Septuagint). It thus makes sense that they came to refer to their communities as *ekklēsia*, as *qahal*, "the assembly of Israel in the new age."[17] Lindbeck spells this out further by developing four heuristic guidelines for reading the New Testament and its references to the church.

First, Lindbeck argues that "early Christian communal self-understanding was narrative-shaped"—they understood themselves first and foremost in light of their story. So, Lindbeck argues terms like "body of Christ" or the marks of the church as "one, holy, catholic, and apostolic" were not defined first and then read into the narrative. Instead, the narrative was "logically prior" and "determined the meaning of the images, concepts, doctrines and theories of the church rather than being determined by them."[18] Connected with this guideline, Lindbeck says that Christians used the term "church" to

---

16. Lindbeck, "The Church," 182.

17. Lindbeck, "The Church," 182–83. Lindbeck forcefully argues, against *Lumen Gentium*, that the church is not the "new people of God," but rather the people of God in the new age. He insists, "The inclusion of the uncircumcised in the covenant with Abraham by means of the new covenant did not, for the earliest Christians, constitute the formation of a different people but rather the enlargement of the old" (185).

18. Lindbeck, "The Church," 183.

refer to "concrete groups of people, not to something transempirical," for "An invisible church is as biblically odd as an invisible Israel."[19] Christian writers like Paul referred to actual, concrete churches, "in all their actual or potential messiness," as "holy" or as the "bride of Christ."[20]

Second, for the earliest Christians, "Israel's history was their only history."[21] They did not yet have a New Testament, and while they read Israel's Scriptures through the lens of Christ, the Old Testament "was the privileged source of the terms, concepts, images and models which they used in understanding Jesus and the Jesus movement to which they belonged."[22] Therefore, "the Old Testament functioned as *the* sole ecclesiological textbook except where it was trumped by the New."[23]

Third, and connected with the second guideline, Christians appropriated all of Israel's story, and not just the accounts of a faithful remnant—"All the wickedness of the Israelites in the wilderness could be theirs."[24] In this context, Lindbeck points to Paul's words in 1 Cor 10:1– 11. There, Paul tells the predominantly Gentile church in Corinth that "our fathers" (RSV) or "our ancestors" (NRSV) were in the wilderness with Moses. They "were all under the cloud, and all passed through the sea, and all were baptized into Moses in the cloud and in the sea, and all ate the same spiritual food, and all drank the same spiritual drink. For they drank from the spiritual rock that followed them, and the rock was Christ" (vv. 1–3). But

19. Lindbeck, "The Church," 183.
20. Lindbeck, "The Church," 183.
21. Lindbeck, "The Church," 183.
22. Lindbeck, "The Gospel's Uniqueness," 434.
23. Lindbeck, "The Church as Israel," 81.
24. Lindbeck, "The Church," 184.

many of them were struck down in the wilderness due to their disobedience. Paul tells them that this occurred as an "example" (NRSV) or a "warning" (RSV)[25] for us, and "they were written down to instruct us" (v. 11). Lindbeck concludes, "The lesson to be drawn from these verses is that for Christians to practice being the church as Israel is for them to apply to their own community what they read about Israel in the *Tanakh*, the Old Testament. More pictorially expressed, it is a matter of seeing the church in the mirror of Old Testament Israel in the light of Jesus Christ."[26]

Fourth, they understood Israel and the church as one covenant people of God. Lindbeck says, "The French remain French after the revolution, the Quakers remain Quakers after becoming wealthy, and Israel remains Israel even when transformed by the arrival of the eschaton in Christ. The church is simply Israel in the time between the times. The continuity of the story and the identity of the people are unbroken."[27] In making this claim, Lindbeck does not argue that the church has replaced or *expropriated* Israel. Instead, he argues that the church should *appropriate* the identity of Israel, or "claim to be Israel without replacing the Jews."[28]

Despite what some in the history of biblical interpretation have presumed, "the relation of Israel's history to that of the church in the New Testament was not that of shadow to reality, or promise to fulfillment, or type to antitype. Jesus Christ alone is the antitype or fulfillment.

---

25. The Greek here is τύποι (*tupoi*) (v. 6) or τυπικῶς (*tupikos*) (v. 11)—"types."

26. Lindbeck, "The Church as Israel," 81.

27. Lindbeck, "The Church," 184.

28. Lindbeck, "Postmodern Hermeneutics," 110.

He is depicted as the embodiment of Israel (e.g., 'Out of Egypt have I called my son', Matt. 2:15), and the church is the body of Christ."[29] Jesus' role is different from that of the people, for "He is redemption itself while they are witnesses."[30] So the relation of the Israel to the church is not one of type to antitype, but rather one of prototype to ectype—original to copy.[31]

Gentile Christians have been grafted into Israel (Rom 11:17–34)—made part of the expanded Israel. The nations, as the prophets foresaw, have come to worship on Mount Zion (Isa 2:3; Mic 4:2; Amos 9:11–12). They function, Krister Stendahl (1921–2008) says, as "honorary Jews."[32] As Paul says to Gentile believers in Eph 2:12–13, "[R]emember that you were at that time without Christ, being aliens from the commonwealth of Israel, and strangers to the covenants of promise, having no hope and without God in the world. But now in Christ Jesus you who once were far off have been brought near by the blood of Christ." It is, therefore, through Christ that Gentiles are brought into the expanded commonwealth of Israel.

While Paul says that unbelieving Jews have been "cut off," he reminds gentile Christians that the same can happen to them. They can, as Revelation 3:16 says, be spit out. They may, as the Northern Kingdom of Israel illustrates, be destroyed. But, at the same time, "this does not alter the unconditionality of the election of those which remain recognizably Jewish or Christian even when they apostatize."[33] As Paul says, "[F]or the gifts and calling of

---

29. Lindbeck, "The Church," 184.
30. Lindbeck, "The Gospel's Uniqueness," 443.
31. Lindbeck, "The Gospel's Uniqueness," 435–36.
32. Stendahl, *Paul Among Jews and Gentiles*, 37.
33. Lindbeck, "The Church," 190.

God are irrevocable" (Rom 11:29).[34] Though the church, like Israel, may act like an adulterous spouse (Ezek 16, 23; Hosea), pursuing other gods, "God does not abrogate his covenant."[35]

This does not mean Lindbeck minimizes the changes that have come in the new age—the Messiah has come, and the Spirit has been poured out in a way it was not before (Acts 2). He affirms, "Whatever is true of Israel is true of the church except where the differences are explicit."[36] Israel maintained its identity in the face of change in the past—Israel looks different in the wilderness than it did under the judges, under the kings, or in exile—so the church can continue to discern what it means to be a part of the expanded Israel in the new age.[37] For example, as leadership structures within Israel shifted to meet new circumstances, then perhaps the church should be open to analogous changes. As leadership in Israel shifted from Shiloh to Jerusalem and then shifted elsewhere after Jerusalem's destruction, perhaps leadership could shift from Rome to another place?

At the same time, however, Lindbeck notes that continuity and tradition are also important within Israel's history, so the church should not simply rely upon

---

34. Lindbeck says, "Looked at in canonical context, God's call and covenant remain unconditional for Israel no matter what its behavior. The rabbinic tradition at least in part agrees with this, but Paul goes further. According to Rom. 11:29 ff., the continuation of God's promises is not ruptured even by Israel's rejection of the Messiah" (Lindbeck, "The Gospel's Uniqueness," 442).

35. Lindbeck, "The Gospel's Uniqueness," 442. In this, Lindbeck applies *simul justus et peccator* to not only individuals but to the church itself. He argues that this move "can be revolutionary for ecclesiology" (Lindbeck, "Response," 206).

36. Lindbeck, "The Church," 183.

37. Lindbeck, "The Church," 192.

pragmatic criteria for its governance. Lindbeck insists, "It is God who guides his people and orders their common life."[38] This is the case even when God reluctantly gives in to Israel's wishes (1 Samuel 8). Just as Lindbeck prefers a *corrective* rather than a *constitutive* perspective on the Reformation,[39] so he prefers "the reform of past structures, not their replacement."[40]

Nor does Lindbeck deny that the New Testament authors appropriated the story of Israel in diverse ways, even within the same author. Paul speaks very differently in 1 Thess 2:14–15 than he does in Romans 9–11. The Johannine literature lacks an emphasis upon the people of God, whereas Hebrews has a "platonized" discussion of the church as a people. Despite these differences, he contends that within a narrative "people-of-God" framework, one can speak of "a basically unified New Testament understanding of the church."[41]

Lindbeck provides four concluding points on the church's identity. First, while he does not deny the importance of faithfulness, he argues "the identity and being of the church rests on God's election, not on its faithfulness."[42] The election of Israel, was unconditional and by grace alone (*sola gratia*). As Deut 7:7 says, "It was not because you were more numerous than any other people that the LORD set his heart on you and chose you—for you were the fewest of all peoples." Yet, God chose Israel and it was because of the oath he made to their ancestors that God set them free from Egypt (v. 8). Lindbeck contends that,

38. Lindbeck, "The Church," 196.
39. See chapter 1.
40. Lindbeck, "The Church," 197.
41. Lindbeck, "The Church," 186.
42. Lindbeck, "The Church," 192.

just as Israel recognizes that God loves them due to his promises to their ancestors, God loves the church not because of its merits "but also because of the ancestors in the faith from Abraham, Sarah, Moses and David, to Teresa of Avila, [Toyohiko] Kagawa, Martin Luther King and John XXIII."[43] When Christian communities identify themselves primarily by their own faithfulness rather than by God's election, "they look for some property within themselves," rather than within God's covenant faithfulness, "that ensures that God will continue to acknowledge them as his own."[44] This has perilous consequences.

Second, God stamps the elect community with certain objective marks. These marks of circumcision or baptism, the Seder or the Lord's Supper, the *shema* or the apostolic teaching, can be either a blessing or a curse depending upon how they are received. As Paul reminds us in 1 Cor 11:29, "all who eat and drink without discerning the body, eat and drink judgment against themselves." Third, while much Christian reflection on election since has focused upon *individual* election, Lindbeck draws upon Jewish theologians like David Novak (1941–) and Michael Wyschogrod (1928–2015) and argues that election is primarily communal: "Individuals are elect by virtue of visible membership in God's people."[45]

Fourth, the primary mission of God's messianic pilgrim people is "to witness to the God who judges and who saves, not to save those who would otherwise be damned."[46] While Rev 7:9 says that people from every nation, tribe,

---

43. Lindbeck, "The Gospel's Uniqueness," 442.

44. Lindbeck, "The Church as Israel," 92.

45. Lindbeck, "The Church," 192. See Novak, *The Election*; Wyschogrod, *The Body*; Lindbeck, "Response," 205.

46. Lindbeck, "The Church," 192.

and language stand before the throne, Lindbeck cautions against saddling outsiders with the burdens of election, for "the possibilities of damnation as well as of salvation are increased within the people of God."[47] One can, for instance, look at the examples of Ananias and Sapphira or Judas to see this. Lindbeck concludes that the Bible does not provide a justification for saying that all those who are not Christians in this life are condemned, though that does not mean that they receive salvation or that they are a part of the kingdom in this life. Lindbeck points here to Jesus' words in Matt 23:15, where he reproaches the scribes and Pharisees for crossing "sea and land to make a single convert," for they "make the new convert twice as much a child of hell as yourselves."[48]

Rather than focus on making converts, Lindbeck calls upon the contemporary church to make disciples—to follow the early church's practice of prolonged catechesis. This does not mean Lindbeck denies the import of Christian mission. The church witnesses to the nations not by saving souls or by trying to improve the social order, but by its communal life—by "being the body of Christ, the communal sign of the promised redemption, in the time between the times."[49] The church is called to be a "servant people,"[50] or what Ephraim Radner (1956–) calls "a nation for the nations, bound to the one purpose of Christ."[51] God elects Abraham in order that all the nations may be blessed (Gen 12:1–3), and Isaiah says that God made a covenant

---

47. Lindbeck, "The Church," 193.

48. See Lindbeck, "The Gospel's Uniqueness," 435. Note that Lindbeck makes this claim as the child of missionaries.

49. Lindbeck, "The Church," 194.

50. Lindbeck, "The Gospel's Uniqueness," 424.

51. Radner, *Church*, 90.

Israelologist

with his people in order that they would be "a light to the nations" (Isa 42:6; cf. Matt 5:14). Through Jeremiah, God tells the people in exile that they should "seek the welfare of the city where I have sent you into exile, and pray to the LORD on its behalf, for in its welfare you will find your welfare" (Jer 29:7). As we see from the story of Israel and the history of the church, faithful witness will sometimes attract disciples, but other times it may lead to persecution and martyrdom, and, as Lindbeck notes, "exactly the same can be said about unfaithfulness."[52]

This conception of the church did not continue as circumstances changed. In a sense, this is understandable. After the destruction of the temple, the church went from consisting of mostly Jews to mostly Gentiles, and given the increasing opposition between the church and the synagogue, it became increasingly difficult for Gentiles to imagine themselves as "naturalized citizens in the continuous, uninterrupted commonwealth of Israel."[53] Patristic documents, like the Epistle of Barnabas, came to "reject the notion that unbelieving Jews remained part of God's people."[54] While early Christians like Paul applied all of Israel's story, even the sinful parts, to the church, Christians began applying Israel-as-remnant to the church and unfaithful Israel to the synagogue.[55] So in this stage, the church moved from *appropriation* of Israel's story to *expropriation*.

Lindbeck argues that despite the baggage that came into the church through this shift, not all was lost. In the

---

52. Lindbeck, "The Gospel's Uniqueness," 446.

53. Lindbeck, "The Church," 187. See also Lindbeck, "The Church as Israel," 83–84.

54. Lindbeck, "The Church," 186.

55. Lindbeck, "The Church as Israel," 91.

second century, Marcion (85–160) argued that the God of Abraham, Isaac, and Jacob—the God revealed in the Old Testament—was not the God and Father of Jesus Christ, but a lesser deity. Marcion contrasted the vengeful God of the Old Testament and the gracious and loving God revealed in Jesus. In so doing, he rejected both the Old Testament as Scripture and the connection between the church and Israel. Many found Marcion's theology appealing. Some scholars estimate that there were just as many Marcionites as catholic Christians for a time. Yet in reaction to the spread of Marcionism, Christians in the middle of the second century began turning in earnest to the Old Testament and, Lindbeck argues, they came to see the church as an Israel-like body. Though they expropriated, rather than appropriated, Israel's identity, Lindbeck argues their readings of Scripture should not be dismissed as unfaithful. He says, "They were the historically (i.e., contingently) necessary conditions for the church's appropriation of Israel's story."[56] Apart from their reading of Scripture, perhaps the views of the Gnostics or the Marcionites would have been universally held by Christians. The Old Testament, typologically and christologically interpreted, brought consensus and community to the early Christian movement's opposition to Marcion. Lindbeck says, "The gentiles who entered this biblical world developed in the course of time a Christian analogue to the Jewish sense of being a single people."[57] This identification of the church with Israel looked different for Tertullian and Cyprian in Carthage than it did

---

56. Lindbeck, "The Church," 187. See Lindbeck, "The Church as Israel," 84–86.

57. Lindbeck, "The Church as Israel," 86.

for Clement and Origen in Alexandria, but both of these streams became a part of the Christian mainstream.[58]

The rise of Constantine continued church-as-Israel discourse, but also sowed "[s]eeds of failure." While Christians previously portrayed emperors as antitypes of Pharaoh, Christians like Eusebius began depicting Constantine as an antitype of Moses, and others later depicted kings and emperors like Charlemagne as Davidic figures. This makes a certain amount of sense, especially since for Christians like Eusebius, persecution was a fresh memory. Lindbeck argues, however, "Once Christianity became, not only licit, but imperially favored, Christians couldn't help but see a very different reflection of themselves in the mirror of Israel."[59] Christians went from being persecuted pilgrims to a persecuting majority, retaliating against the pagans and Jews. Words they previously used as "cries of anguish in the mouths of the helpless became incitements to violence against the newly defenseless when repeated from positions of strength."[60]

In the later medieval period, the churches moved from expropriation to neglect—they no longer focused upon the church as Israel. In the Reformation and the ensuing "wars of religion," conflicting Christian parties in Europe renewed the utilization of Israel discourse, but in it Protestants and Catholics bickered over which was the Northern and Southern Kingdoms of Israel, with both sides claiming they were prefigured by Judah and are the "true New Israel."[61] In the modern period, various Christian communities, both Catholic and Protestant—not only

58. Lindbeck, "The Church as Israel," 82.
59. Lindbeck, "The Church as Israel," 88.
60. Lindbeck, "The Church as Israel," 88.
61. Lindbeck, "The Church as Israel," 89.

ceased to refer to the church as Israel, but they dropped the concept of the church's Israelhood altogether. They no longer looked to Israel's story to understand the church, but instead looked exclusively to Acts or Paul's letters. Some, like Friedrich Schleiermacher, renewed a "rejectionist understanding of the relation of Christianity to Judaism."[62] Ecclesiologists later came to abandon "the referential primacy of empirical communities."[63] They came to treat predicates of the church, such as "event, or mission, or liberating action, or the new being in Christ, or the fellowship of the Spirit, or the communion of Christ's justifying grace," as subjects, and saw empirical churches as imperfect manifestations of these predicates.[64]

Lindbeck argues that in many ways, the present period is more like the time of Christian beginnings than any time in between. He says, "Christendom is passing and Christians are becoming a diaspora."[65] So perhaps now is the time to retrieve the church's identity as Israel. He acknowledges, however, that some reject this option outright, and perhaps for good reason. The notion that the church is "true Israel" often went hand in hand with the belief that God has rejected the Jews, and these two ideas together contributed to centuries of Christian anti-Semitism and the Holocaust. It is for this reason that Lindbeck provides certain conditions, such as his distinction between appropriation and expropriation, within his proposal. In this, he seeks to describe the church as Israel in a non-supersessionist way.[66]

62. Lindbeck, "The Church as Israel," 90.
63. Lindbeck, "The Church," 188.
64. Lindbeck, "The Church," 189.
65. Lindbeck, "The Church," 190.
66. Lindbeck, "The Church as Israel," 79–80.

Israelologist

As noted previously, Linbeck argues that this way of describing the church has ecumenical potential. He says, "The church thus identified sounds Catholic in its comprehensiveness, Calvinist in the unconditionality of its chosenness, and Lutheran in its possibilities of unfaithfulness while remaining genuinely the church; but the total effect, not surprisingly, is more Jewish than anything else."[67]

Lindbeck concludes that the retrieval of ecclesial Israelhood has three ecumenical consequences. First, Christians can come to understand that they are not called to be a part of God's people primarily for their own individual salvation, but "in order to contribute to the world's redemption by their membership in the body of Christ, the enlarged Israel, which God has unconditionally chosen to be his light to the nations for the redemption of the world."[68] Second, identification with Israel allows for the possibility of communal repentance—both for intra-Christian disunity and for Christianity disunity with the Jewish people. While ecumenical discourse can often lead Christians to accept separated Christian existence as normative, by looking at the church in the mirror of Israel the church can "as a whole learn how to lament biblically for its intramural and extramural divisiveness and lovelessness."[69] Third, within an understanding of the church as Israel, individuals are called to help the churches become penitent. They do so by "suffering and rejoicing on behalf of the church."[70] Like Israel's prophets, they may

67. Lindbeck, "The Church," 192–93.

68. Lindbeck, "The Church as Israel," 93.

69. Lindbeck, "The Church as Israel," 94.

70. Lindbeck, "The Church as Israel," 94. See 1 Cor 12:26 and Col 1:24.

call the people to repentance while also remaining loyal to God and God's people.

DOXOLOGY

Lindbeck has issues related to worship in mind as well. He explains, "Let us assume in agreement with rabbinic and Christian scriptural interpretation that the basic response which God desires from those whom he elects, and ultimately from all, is praise, doxology, joy in God and God's creation."[71] Lindbeck argues that while some twentieth-century Christian theologians have made doxology central to their theological projects, Jews have often maintained this emphasis more than Christians: "The rabbis frequently urge, for example, that the primary response God wants is not gratitude: it is self-centered to respond to God only because of the good he has done us."[72] While 1 John 4:19 says, "We love because he first loved us," Bernard of Clairvaux (1090–1153) affirms that we should seek to love God not just because of what he has done for us, but for God's own sake. And we express this love as praise.

Similarly, as the rabbis affirmed, we should obey God not simply for some instrumental reason but because obedience to God's commands is its own reward, and "for that reason meritorious, virtue-producing, and neighbor-benefiting."[73] He concludes, "God's self-communication occurs in and through the church's liturgical, communal and diakonal practices as these are done for their own sake in praise of God, not for some extrinsic good.

---

71. Lindbeck, "The Gospel's Uniqueness," 445.
72. Lindbeck, "The Gospel's Uniqueness," 445.
73. Lindbeck, "The Gospel's Uniqueness," 446.

Faithful witness is doxology and *vice versa*."[74] In this he compares the relation of doxology to obedience to the way the Reformers compared faith and works: "the second is a necessary by, in one sense, accidental by-product of the former."[75]

CONCLUSION

Lindbeck contends that a reevaluation of the relation of the church to Israel is imperative for Christian ecumenism. He provides such an account while avoiding the trap of supersessionism, the view that God has rejected the Jews and that Christians are now the true Israel.[76] He leaves it up to Jews to decide whether or not a non-supersessionist understanding of the church as Israel holds promise. He holds out hope that they will by pointing to Jacob Neusner, who says, "The Church long ago identified itself as Israel and, through the shared Scriptures, with Israel. In our day, all the more so, the Church joins suffering Israel."[77] Lindbeck concludes, "To this I would add only the obvious comment that the church can do this only by learning to see itself once again in the mirror of Israel while, in contrast to the past, fully acknowledging that the covenant with the Jews has not been revoked."[78]

Lindbeck hoped to produce a book on his work on the church as Israel,[79] but unfortunately he had a brain aneurism in 2009 that prevented him from completing

---

74. Lindbeck, "The Gospel's Uniqueness," 446.
75. Lindbeck, "The Gospel's Uniqueness," 446.
76. See also Soulen, *The God*, 30–32.
77. Neusner, *Christian Faith*, xiv.
78. Lindbeck, "The Church as Israel," 94.
79. Lindbeck, "Paris," 405–08.

the project.⁸⁰ Upon his death on January 8, 2018, several reflections by friends, colleagues, former students, and admirers were published in publications and websites from across the theological spectrum, such as *Living Church*, *Pro Ecclesia*, *First Things*, *Commonweal*, *Christian Century*, and *Christianity Today*.⁸¹ These various articles and essays reflect upon Lindbeck as a person, as well as upon his work as a teacher, an observer at Vatican II, and an ecumenist. Bruce Marshall says, "When news reached me that he had died after a long illness, among my first thoughts was that when people remembered him as a theologian, he would have liked it to be as a servant of Christian unity."⁸²

Discussion Questions

1. How does the narrative of Scripture determine our understanding of the church?

2. Lindbeck points to 1 Cor 10:1–11 as particularly important for ecclesiological reflection. What does this passage help us understand about the church and its relation to Israel?

3. How should we reconcile the diverse ways that the New Testament authors refer to the church (and the Jews)?

4. What is election?

---

80. Sterling, "George Lindbeck." In that obituary, his daughter Kris notes that despite that, "he would brighten during her visits to the assisted living center in Florida where he spent his final years, where she would read him scripture and other Christian writings."

81. I mentioned and engaged with several of these pieces earlier in the volume.

82. Marshall, "Discovering Agreement," 10.

Israelologist

5. What is the mission of the church?
6. What are the ecumenical benefits of seeing the church as Israel?
7. What implications does Lindbeck's Israelology have for the doctrine of God?

BIBLIOGRAPHY

Anderson, H. George, T. Austin Murphy, and Joseph A. Burgess, eds. *Justification by Faith*. Lutherans and Catholics in Dialogue 7. Minneapolis: Augsburg, 1985.

Bauerschmidt, Frederick Christian. *Holy Teaching: Introducing the Summa Theologiae of St. Thomas Aquinas*. Grand Rapids: Brazos, 2005.

The Book of Concord: Confessions of the Evangelical Lutheran Church. Translated and edited by Theodore G. Tappert. Philadelphia: Fortress, 1959.

Brown, Shaun C. *George Lindbeck and the Israel of God*. Pathways for Ecumenical and Interreligious Dialogue. London: Palgrave Macmillan, 2021.

Buckley James J. "Introduction: Radical Traditions: Evangelical, Catholic and Postliberal." In *The Church in a Postliberal Age*, by George Lindbeck, edited by James J. Buckley, vii–xviii. Radical Traditions: Theology in a Postcritical Key. Grand Rapids: Eerdmans, 2002.

Burrell, David B. *Aquinas: God and Action*. 3rd ed. Eugene, OR: Wipf & Stock, 2016.

Calhoun, Robert L. "The Role of Historical Theology." *Journal of Religion* 21, no. 4 (October 1941) 444–54.

———. *Scripture, Creed, Theology: Lectures on the History of Christian Doctrine in the First Centuries*. Edited by George Lindbeck. Eugene, OR: Cascade, 2011.

Casarella, Peter. "Mr. Lindbeck's Surprisingly Effective Pedagogy and Its Consequences for Today." *Pro Ecclesia* 27, no. 4 (Fall 2018) 369–75.

Bibliography

Congar, Yves. *Divided Christendom: A Catholic Study of the Problem of Reunion*. Translated by M.A. Bousfield. London: Centenary, 1939.

Congrove, Caleb. "*Fides caritate formata*." *Living Church* (February 18, 2018) 29.

"Constitution on the Sacred Liturgy: *Sacrosanctum Concilium*." In *Vatican Council II: The Basic Sixteen Documents: Constitutions, Decrees, Declarations: A Completely Revised Translation in Inclusive Language*, edited by by Austin Flannery, 117–61. Collegeville: Liturgical, 2014.

"Decree On Ecumenism: *Unitatis Redintegratio*." In *Vatican Council II: The Basic Sixteen Documents: Constitutions, Decrees, Declarations: A Completely Revised Translation in Inclusive Language*, edited by by Austin Flannery, 499–523. Collegeville: Liturgical, 2014.

"Dogmatic Constitution on the Church: *Lumen Gentium*." In *Vatican Council II: The Basic Sixteen Documents: Constitutions, Decrees, Declarations: A Completely Revised Translation in Inclusive Language*, edited by by Austin Flannery, 1–95. Collegeville: Liturgical, 2014.

"Dogmatic Constitution on Divine Revelation: *Dei Verbum*." In *Vatican Council II: The Basic Sixteen Documents: Constitutions, Decrees, Declarations: A Completely Revised Translation in Inclusive Language*, edited by by Austin Flannery, 97–115. Collegeville: Liturgical, 2014.

Eckerstorfer, Bernhard A. "The One Church in the Postmodern World: Reflections on the Life and Thought of George Lindbeck." *Pro Ecclesia* 13, no. 4 (Fall 2004) 399–423.

Frei, Hans W. *The Eclipse of Biblical Narrative: A Study in Eighteenth and Nineteenth Century Hermeneutics*. New Haven: Yale University Press, 1974.

———. "The 'Literal Reading' of Biblical Narrative in the Christian Tradition: Does It Stretch or Will It Break?" In *The Bible and the Narrative Tradition*, edited by Frank McConnell, 36–77. Oxford: Oxford University Press, 1986.

———. *Types of Christian Theology*. Edited by George Hunsinger and William C. Placher. New Haven: Yale University Press, 1992.

Frye, Northrop. *The Great Code: The Bible and Literature*. Toronto: Academic Press Canada, 1972.

Gafney, Wilda C. *Womanist Midrash: A Reintroduction to the Women of the Torah and the Throne*. Louisville: Westminster John Knox Press, 2017.

Bibliography

Geertz, Clifford. *The Interpretation of Cultures*. New York: Basic Books, 1973.

Granfield, Patrick. "George Lindbeck." In *Theologians at Work*, 151–64. New York: MacMillan, 1967.

Eckhart, Adam, Christine Luckritz, George Keddie, and Martha Lund Smalley. "Guide to the George A. Lindbeck Papers." *Archives at Yale*, 2014. https://archives.yale.edu/repositories/4/resources/130.

Helmer, Christine. *How Luther Became the Reformer*. Louisville: Westminster John Knox, 2019.

Higton, Mike. "Forward." In *The Identity of Jesus Christ: The Hermeneutical Bases of Dogmatic Theology*, by Hans W. Frei, xi–xix. Updated and expanded ed. Eugene, OR: Cascade, 2013.

———. "Reconstructing 'The Nature of Doctrine.'" *Modern Theology* 30, no. 1 (January 2014) 1–31.

Jenson, Robert. "On Recognizing the Augsburg Confession." In *The Role of the Augsburg Confession*, edited by Joseph A. Burgess, 151–66. Philadelphia: Fortress, 1980.

Kelsey, David H. *Proving Doctrine: The Uses of Scripture in Modern Theology*. Harrisburg: Trinity Press International, 1999.

Kilby, Karen. "Ecumenical Generosity." *Commonweal* (March 23, 2018) 6, 8.

Leo XIII. *Aeterni Patris*. Enyclical letter. August 4, 1879. http://www.vatican.va/content/leo-xiii/en/encyclicals/documents/hf_l-xiii_enc_04081879_aeterni-patris.html.

Lindbeck, George. "Abelard, Peter." *American Peoples Encyclopedia*. New York: Grolier, 1965.

———. "Article IV and Lutheran/Roman Catholic Dialogue: The Limits of Diversity in the Understanding of Justification." *Lutheran Theological Seminary Bulletin* 61, no. 1 (Winter 1981) 3–16.

———. "Catholicisme Américain." *La Semeur* 46 (1947) 274–81.

———. "The Church." In *Keeping the Faith: Essays to Mark the Centenary of Lux Mundi*, edited by Geoffrey Wainwright, 179–208. Philadelphia: Fortress, 1988.

———. "The Church as Israel: Ecclesiology and Ecumenism." In *Jews and Christians: People of God*, edited by Carl E. Braaten and Robert W. Jenson, 78–94. Grand Rapids: Eerdmans, 2003.

———. "The Church's Mission in a Postmodern World." In *Postmodern Theology: Christian Faith in a Pluralist World*, edited by Frederic B. Burnham, 37–55. San Francisco: Harper & Row, 1989.

Bibliography

———. "Confession and Community: An Israel-like View of the Church." *Christian Century* 107, no. 16 (May 9, 1990) 492–96.

———. "Confessional Faithfulness and the Ecumenical Future: The J.L. Neve Memorial Lecture." *Trinity Seminary Review* 12 (1990) 59–66.

———. "Confessional Subscription: What Does It Mean for Lutherans Today?" *Word & World* 11, no. 3 (Summer 1991) 19–20, 317.

———. "The Crisis in American Catholicism." In *Our Common History as Christians: Essays in Honor of Albert C. Outler*, edited by John Deschner, Leroy T. Howe, and Klaus Penzel, 47–66. New York: Oxford University Press, 1975.

———. "The Crucial Role of the American Church." *Lutheran Forum* 41, no. 1 (1980) 8–10.

———. "Discovering Thomas (1): The Classical Statement of Christian Theism." *Una Sancta* 24, no. 1 (1967) 45–52.

———. "Discovering Thomas (2): Tentative Language about the Trinity." *Una Sancta* 24, no. 3 (1967) 44–48.

———. "Discovering Thomas (3): The Origin of Man." *Una Sancta* 24, no. 4 (1967) 67–75.

———. "Discovering Thomas (4): Hope and the Sola Fide." *Una Sancta* 25, no. 1 (1968) 66–73.

———, ed. *Dialogue on the Way: Protestant Report from Rome on the Vatican Council*. Minneapolis: Augsburg, 1965.

———. "Ecumenical Directions and Confessional Construals." *Dialog* 30 (1991) 118–23.

———. "Erickson's Young Man Luther: A Historical and Theological Reappraisal." *Soundings* 56, no. 2 (Summer 1973) 210–27.

———. "Foreword to the German Edition of 'The Nature of Doctrine.'" In *The Nature of Doctrine: Religion and Theology in a Postliberal Age*, xxix–xxxii. 25th ann. ed. Louisville: Westminster John Knox, 2009.

———. *The Future of Roman Catholic Theology*. Philadelphia: Fortress, 1970.

———. "The Gospel's Uniqueness: Election and Untranslatability." *Modern Theology* 13, no. 4 (October 1997) 423–50.

———. *Infallibility*. Pere Marquette Theology Lecture. Milwaukee: Marquette University Press, 1972.

———. "The Infallibility Debate." In *The Infallibility Debate*, edited by John J. Kirvan, 107–52. New York: Paulist, 1971.

———. "Introduction: Calhoun as Historical Theologian." In *Scripture, Creed, Theology: Lectures on the History of Christian*

Bibliography

Doctrine in the First Centuries, by Robert L. Calhoun, edited by George Lindbeck, ix–lxx. Eugene, OR: Cascade, 2011.

———. "Jewish-Christian Dialogue." *Journal of Ecumenical Studies* 3 (1966) 146–47.

———. "The Jews, Renewal, and Ecumenism." *Journal of Ecumenical Studies* 2 (1965) 471–73.

———. "John Courtney Murray, S.J.: An Evaluation." *Christianity and Crisis* 21 (1961) 213–16.

———. "Karl Rahner and a Protestant View of the Sacramentality of the Ministry." *Proceedings of the Catholic Theological Society of America* 21 (1966) 267–88.

———. "Luther on Law in Ecumenical Context." *Dialog* 22 (1983) 270–74.

———. "Lutheran Churches." In *Ministry in America: A Report and Analysis, Based on an In-Depth Survey of 47 Denominations in the United States and Canada, with Interpretation by 18 Experts*, edited by David S. Schuller, Merton P. Strommen, and Milo L. Brekke, 414–44. San Francisco: Harper & Row, 1980.

———. "Lutheranism as Church & Movement: Trends in America since 1980." *Lutheran Theological Seminary Bulletin* 71, no. 1 (1991) 43–59.

———. "Martin Luther and the Rabbinic Mind." In *Understanding the Rabbinic Mind: Essays on the Hermeneutic of Max Kadushin*, edited by Peter Ochs, 141–64. South Florida Studies in the History of Judaism 14. Atlanta: Scholars, 1990.

———. "Modernity and Luther's Understanding of the Freedom of the Christian." In *Martin Luther and the Modern Mind: Freedom, Conscience, Toleration, Rights*, edited by Manfred Hoffman, 1–22. Toronto Studies in Theology 22. New York/Toronto: Edwin Mellen, 1985.

———. *The Nature of Doctrine: Religion and Theology in a Postliberal Age*. 25th ann. ed. Louisville: Westminster John Knox, 2009.

———. "Nominalism and the Problem of Meaning as Illustrated by Pierre d'Ailly on Predestination and Justification." *Harvard Theological Review* 52 (1959) 43–60.

———. "Non-Theological Factors and Structures of Unity." In *Einheit der Kirche: Neue Entwicklungen und Perspektiven*, edited by Gunther Gassmann and Peder Nørgaard-Højen, 133–45. Frankfurt: Lembeck, 1988.

———. "A Note on Aristotle's Discussion of God and World." *Review of Metaphysics* 2 (1948) 99–106.

Bibliography

———. "Papacy and *Ius Divinum*: A Lutheran View." In *Papal Primacy and the Universal Church*, edited by Paul C. Empire and T. Austin Murphy, 193–208. Lutherans and Catholics in Dialogue V. Minneapolis: Augsburg, 1974.

———. "Paris, Rome, Jerusalem: An Ecumenical Journey." *Journal of Ecumenical Studies* 41, no. 3–4 (Summer–Fall 2004) 389–408.

———. "Postmodern Hermeneutics and Jewish-Christian Dialogue: A Case Study." In *Christianity in Jewish Terms*, edited by Tikva Frymer-Kensky, David Novak, Peter Ochs, David Fox Sandmel, and Michael A. Signer, 106–13. Boulder: Westview, 2000.

———. "Problems on the Road to Unity: Infallibility." In *Unitatis Redintegratio: 1964-1974-Eine Bilanz Der Auswirkungen Des Ökumenismusdekrets*, edited by Gerard Békés and Vilmos Vajta, 98–109. Studia Anselmiana 71. Frankfurt: Lembeck/Knecht, 1977.

———. "Protestant Problems with Lonergan on Development of Dogma." In *Foundations of Theology: Papers from the International Lonergan Congress 1970*, edited by Philip McShane, SJ, 115–23. Notre Dame,: University of Notre Dame Press, 1972.

———. "A Protestant View of the Ecclesiological Status of the Roman Catholic Church." *Journal of Ecumenical Studies* 1, no. 2 (Spring 1964) 243–70.

———. "A Question of Compatibility: A Lutheran Reflects on Trent." In *Justification by Faith*, edited by H. George Anderson, T. Austin Murphy, and Joseph A. Burgess, 230–40. Lutherans and Catholics in Dialogue 7. Minneapolis: Augsburg, 1985.

———. "Reform and Infallibility." *Cross Currents* 11 (1961) 213–16.

———. "The Reformation Heritage and Christian Unity." *Lutheran Quarterly* 2, no. 4 (Winter 1988) 477–502.

———. "Response to Michael Wyschogrod's 'Letter to a Friend.'" *Modern Theology* 11, no. 2 (April 1995) 205–10.

———. "Roman Catholicism on the Eve of the Council." In *The Papal Council and the Gospel: Protestant Theologians Evaluate the Coming Council*, edited by Kristen E. Skydsgaard, 61–92. Minneapolis: Augsburg, 1961.

———. "The Sectarian Future of the Church." In *The God Experience: Essays in Hope*, edited by Joseph Whelan, 226–42. New York: Newman, 1971.

———. "Scripture, Consensus, and Community." In *Biblical Interpretation in Crisis: The Ratzinger Conference on Bible and Church*, edited by Richard John Neuhaus, 74–101. Grand Rapids: Eerdmans, 1989.

———. "Should the U.S. Send Ambassador to Vatican?" *Foreign Policy Bulletin* 31, no. 7 (1951) 4, 6.

———. "The Story-Shaped Church: Critical Exegesis and Theological Interpretation." In *Scriptural Authority and Narrative Interpretation*, edited by Garrett Green, 161–78. Philadelphia: Fortress, 1987.

———. "Thomism." In *Handbook of Christian Theology: Definition Essays on Concepts and Movements of Thought in Contemporary Protestantism*, edited by Marvin Halverson and Arthur A. Cohen, 361–63. New York: Meridian, 1958.

———. "Thomism—Barrier or Bridge." *Our Sunday Visitor* (November 20, 1960) 2A–3A.

———. "Review Essay: 'Unbaptized God: The Basic Flaw in Ecumenical Theology,' by Robert W. Jenson, 1992." *Pro Ecclesia* 3, no. 2 (Spring 1994) 232–38.

Lindbeck, George, and Vilmos Vajta. "The Augsburg Confession in Light of Contemporary Catholic-Lutheran Dialogue." In *The Role of the Augsburg Confession: Catholic and Lutheran Views*, edited by Joseph A. Burgess, 81–94. Philadelpha: Fortress, 1980.

Livingston, James C., and Francis Schüssler Fiorenza. *Modern Christian Thought: The Twentieth Century*. 2nd ed. Minneapolis: Fortress, 2006.

Luther, Martin. "A Brief Instruction on What to Look For and Expect in the Gospels." In *Martin Luther's Basic Theological Writings*, edited by Timothy F. Lull and William R. Russell, 71–75. 3rd ed. Minneapolis: Fortress, 2012.

———. "*Contra Latomus*." In Vol. 32, *Luther's Works*, translated by George Lindbek, 133–266. Philadelphia: Muhlenberg, 1958.

———. "A Practical Way to Pray." In *Martin Luther's Basic Theological Writings*, edited by Timothy F. Lull and William R. Russell, 33–38. 3rd ed. Minneapolis: Fortress, 2012.

———. "Small Catechism." In *Martin Luther's Basic Theological Writings*, edited by Timothy F. Lull and William R. Russell, 322–39. 3rd ed. Minneapolis: Fortress, 2012.

MacIntyre, Alasdair. *Whose Justice? Which Rationality?* Notre Dame: University of Notre Dame Press, 1988.

Mangina, Joseph. "Charitable Reading, Patience, and the Ecumenical Long Game." *Living Church* (February 18, 2018) 27–28.

Manni, Franco. *Herbert McCabe: Recollecting a Fragmented Legacy*. Eugene, OR: Cascade, 2020.

Marshall, Bruce D. "Absorbing the World: Christianity and the Universe of Truths." In *Theology and Dialogue: Essays in*

Bibliography

Conversation with George Lindbeck, edited by Bruce D. Marshall, 69–102. Notre Dame: University of Notre Dame Press, 1990.

———. "Discovering Agreement." *Christian Century* (February 14, 2018) 10–11.

———. "Introduction: *The Nature of Doctrine* after 25 Years." In *The Nature of Doctrine: Religion and Theology in a Postliberal Age*, by George Lindbeck, vii–xxvii. 25th ann. ed. Louisville: Westminster John Knox Press, 2009.

McCabe, Herbert. *God Matters*. Rev. ed. Woonsocket: Mowbray, 2000.

McKim, Donald K. *The Westminster Dictionary of Theological Terms*. 2nd ed. Louisville: Westminster John Knox Press, 2014.

Michener, Ronald T. *Postliberal Theology: A Guide for the Perplexed*. London: Bloomsbury T&T Clark, 2013.

Neusner, Jacob. *Christian Faith and the Bible of Judaism: The Judaic Encounter with Scripture*. Grand Rapids: Eerdmans, 1987.

Newbigin, Lesslie. *The Household of God: Lectures on the Nature of the Church*. London: SCM, 1953.

Niebuhr, H. Richard. *The Social Sources of Denominationalism*. New York: Holt, 1929.

Novak, David. *The Election of Israel: The Idea of the Chosen People*. Cambridge: Cambridge University Press, 1995.

Ochs, Peter. *Another Reformation: Postliberal Christianity and the Jews*. Grand Rapids: Baker Academic, 2011.

O'Regan, Cyril. "Quintessential, Ecumenical, Lutheran." *Living Church* (February 18, 2018) 25–26.

"Pastoral Constitution on the Church in the Modern World: 'Gaudium et Spes.'" In *Vatican Council II: The Basic Sixteen Documents: Constitutions, Decrees, Declarations: A Completely Revised Translation in Inclusive Language*, edited by Austin Flannery, 163–282. Collegeville: Liturgical, 2014.

"Performing the Faith: An Interview with George Lindbeck." *Christian Century* (November 28, 2006) 28–35.

Phillips, Timothy R., and Dennis L. Okholm, eds. "A Panel Discussion: Lindbeck, Hunsinger, McGrath & Fackre." In *The Nature of Confession: Evangelicals & Postliberals in Conversation*, 246–53. Downers Grove: InterVarsity, 1996.

Pius X. *Doctoris Angelici*. Enyclical letter. June 29, 1914. https://maritain.nd.edu/jmc/etext/doctoris.htm.

Preller, Victor. *Divine Science and the Science of God: A Reformulation of Thomas Aquinas*. Princeton: Princeton University Press, 1967.

Quanbeck, Warren A., ed. *Challenge . . . and Response: A Protestant Perspective of the Vatican Council*. Minneapolis: Augsburg, 1966.

Bibliography

Radner, Ephraim. *Church*. Eugene, OR: Cascade, 2017.

———. "Quiet, Modest Pioneer." *Living Church* (February 18, 2018) 21–23.

Reno, R.R. "George Lindbeck." *First Things* (March 2018) 66–68.

Root, Michael. "Humble and Focused." *Living Church* (February 18, 2018) 29.

Skydsgaard, Kristen E., ed. *The Papal Council and the Gospel: Protestant Theologians Evaluating the Coming Council*. Minneapolis: Augsburg, 1961.

Soulen, R. Kendall. *The God of Israel and Christian Theology*. Minneapolis: Fortress, 1996.

Sterling, Gregory. "Gregory Lindbeck, 1923–2018." *Yale Divinity School*, January 19, 2018. https://divinity.yale.edu/news/george-lindbeck-1923-2018.

Tanner, Norman P., ed. *Decrees of the Ecumenical Councils Volume II: Trent to Vatican II*. London: Sheed & Ward, 1990.

Thomas Aquinas. *Summa Theologiae Prima Pars, 1–49*. Latin/English Edition of the Works of St. Thomas Aquinas 13. Edited by John Mortensen and Enrique Alarcon. Translated by Laurence Shapcote. Lander: Aquinas Institute for the Study of Sacred Doctrine, 2012.

Thomas Aquinas. *Summa Theologiae Secunda Sedundae, 1–91*. Latin/English Edition of the Works of St. Thomas Aquinas 17. Edited by John Mortensen and Enrique Alarcon. Translated by Laurence Shapcote. Lander: Aquinas Institute for the Study of Sacred Doctrine, 2012.

Weigel, George. "Re-Viewing Vatican II: An Interview with George A. Lindbeck." *First Things* (December 1994) 44–50.

Wittgenstein, Ludwig. *Philosophical Investigations*. Edited by P.M.S. Hacker and Joachim Schulte. Translated by G.E.M. Anscombe, P.M.S. Hacker, and Joachim Schulte. 4th ed. Oxford: Wiley-Blackwell, 2009.

Wright, John. "'I Pray That They Might Be One as We Are One': An Interview with George Lindbeck." In *Postliberal Theology and the Church Catholic: Conversations with George Lindbeck, David Burrell, and Stanley Hauerwas*, 55–75. Grand Rapids: Baker Academic, 2012.

———. "Israel, Judgment, and the Future of the Church Catholic: A Dialogue Among Friends." In *Postliberal Theology and the Church Catholic: Conversations with George Lindbeck, David Burrell, and Stanley Hauerwas*, 113–32. Grand Rapids: Baker Academic, 2012.

Bibliography

———. "The Silent Shifting of Tectonic Plates." In *Postliberal Theology and the Church Catholic: Conversations with George Lindbeck, David Burrell, and Stanley Hauerwas*, 11–53. Grand Rapids: Baker Academic, 2012.

"Writings of George A. Lindbeck." In *Theology and Dialogue: Essays in Conversation with George Lindbeck*, edited by Bruce D. Marshall, 283–98. Notre Dame: University of Notre Dame Press, 1990.

Wyschogrod, Michael. *The Body of Faith: God in the People Israel*. 1st Jason Aronson Inc. ed. Lanham: Jason Aronson, 1996.

INDEX OF NAMES

Abelard, 39
Aristotle, 39, 44
Augustine, 44, 100–101, 120, 122
Barth, Karl, 27, 37, 42, 51–52, 54, 124
Bauerschmidt, Frederick Christian, x
Bellarmine, Robert, 63
Bernard of Clairvaux, 150
Bonhoeffer, Dietrich, 18
Brunner, Peter, 6
Buckley, James J., vii, x–xi
Burrell, David, 48
Calhoun, Robert L., 26, 31–34
Calvin, John, 8, 10, 41–42
Charlemagne, 30, 147
Clement of Alexandria, 147
Congar, Yves, 1, 36–37, 58n3, 122n66
Constantine, 147
Cyprian, 146
Daniélou, Jean, 35–37
de Lubac, Henri, 36n39, 122n66
Ebeling, Gerhard, 103
Edwards, Jonathan, 41
Eusebius, 147

Frei, Hans, 33–34, 117, 120–24, 126n82, 130n91
Gafney, Wilda, 16n52
Geertz, Clifford, 31n18, 105, 117–20
Gilson, Étienne, 26, 34
Gritsch, Eric W., 11
Hamilton, H. F., 136
Hauerwas, Stanley, 109
Helmer, Christine, 106n72
Hooker, Richard, 41
Jenson, Robert, 11, 94, 103
Jesus, 28, 30, 49, 51–52, 65, 69, 78, 98, 101, 103, 106, 115, 120, 123–24, 134, 138–40, 144, 146
John Duns Scotus, 34, 39
Kadushin, Max, 15
Kasper, Walter, 79
Kelsey, David, 123–24
Kierkegaard, Søren, 18, 27
Kilby, Karen, ix
Koesters, Reinhard, 99,
Küng, Hans, 76
Lewis, C. S., 1
Lonergan, Bernard, 89, 111–12,
Luther, Martin, 2, 4–5, 9–11, 13–21, 23–24, 39,

165

Index of Names

Luther, Martin (*continued*) 41–43, 55, 70, 93n26, 94, 96–102, 104–5, 106n72, 127
MacIntyre, Alasdair, 8, 109, 126–27n82
Marcion, 146
Maritain, Jacques, 26
Marshall, Bruce, vii, ix, xi–xiin6, 39–40, 54, 82n109, 120n59, 133, 152
McCabe, Herbert, 48
McKim, Donald, 16n52, 18n61
Melanchthon, Philip, 53–54, 96, 100
Murray, John Courtney, 34
Neusner, Jacob, 151,
Newbigin, Lesslie, 136
Newman, John Henry, 80n100
Niebuhr, H. Richard, 26–31, 38
Niebuhr, Reinhold, 27
Novak, David, vii, 143
O'Regan, Cyril, 2, 40n8
Origen, 29, 32, 147
Pawley, Bernard, 59n8
Pesch, Otto, 96, 99n47
Piepkorn, Arthur Carl, 6
Pierre d'Ailly, 39

Pope John XXIII, 57–59, 143
Pope Leo XIII, 40
Pope Pius X, 40
Preller, Victor, 48
Pseudo-Dionysius, 63
Quanbeck, Warren, 59, 60n11
Radner, Ephraim, vii, 144
Rahner, Karl, 51–52, 76, 79, 90, 98, 111
Reichelt, K. L., 6
Ryle, Gilbert, 117
Schillebeeckx, Edward, 98
Schleiermacher, Friedrich, 41, 111, 120, 148
Schlink, Edmund, 6, 59, 96
Sertillanges, A. G., 48
Skydsgaard, Kristen E., 6, 57–59
Tertullian, 32, 146
Thomas Aquinas, xi, 13, 36n39, 39–55, 63n24, 89, 98, 100, 104, 120, 127–28
Tillich, Paul, 41–42
Troeltsch, Ernst, 27–29
Vajta, Vilmos, 59, 91n22
Vignaux, Paul, 26n4, 35
Weber, Max, 28–29, 31
Wittgenstein, Ludwig, 49–50, 89, 105
Wyschogrod, Michael, 143
Zwingli, Ulrich, 10

INDEX OF SUBJECTS

aggiornamento, 83, 90
amidah, 15
analogia entis, 42
antifoundationalism, nonfoundationalism, 126–27
anti-Judaism, 15, 21, 23–24
anti-Semitism, 15, 148
apologetics, 116, 126–29
Aristotelianism, 45, 50–52, 98, 120
Augsburg Confession, 9–10, 12, 76, 91–92, 95, 98–99, 101–2
Augustinianism, 42, 44, 93n26
baptism, 4–6, 15, 87, 95, 143
bishops, 29, 57, 64n29, 74–76, 91
Calvinism, 119, 149
canon of Scripture, 29, 47, 90, 120–21, 123, 141n34
catechesis, catechism(s), 84, 103, 128–29, 144
China, x, 2–5, 25, 34, 129n87
Christendom, 3, 30, 40, 108–9n9
circumcision, 15, 143

cognitive-propositionalism, 110, 112
collegiality, 75
comparative dogmatics, 108–9n9, 133–34
Council of Trent, 91–99
covenant, 65, 137n17, 139–41, 143–45, 151
creeds, 9, 15–16, 18–19, 29, 49, 113–14, 130, 135–36
cultural-linguistic, 3, 105, 112–13, 116, 126, 128–29
de deo trino (see Trinity)
de deo uno (see oneness of God)
Decalogue (see Ten Commandments)
diakonia (see service)
disciples, discipleship, 65, 144–45
doctrine(s), xi, 11–12, 17, 19, 29, 31–33, 46, 55, 75–76, 79, 80n100, 92–94, 96, 100, 102–3, 105–15, 131, 153
dogma(s), 6, 11, 16–17, 24, 32, 41, 58, 61, 78–80,

167

Index of Subjects

dogma(s) (*continued*)
    82, 84, 89, 105, 107, 108–9n9, 114n31, 116, 133–34
doxology, see worship
Eastern Orthodoxy, 6n16, 7n19, 11, 73, 74n77, 80n100, 87, 98, 110
ecclesiology, 10, 134–36, 141n35
ecumenism, ecumenical movement, x–xi, 1–4, 9, 11, 23, 30, 33, 35–36, 38, 40, 54–55, 71–74, 76, 82, 85–111, 131, 134–36, 149, 151, 153
elect(ion), 12, 65, 134, 140, 142–44, 150, 152
episcopacy, see bishops
eschatology, 62–63
ethnography, 117–20
Eucharist, 3, 15, 68, 70, 110–11, 114, 143
experiential-expressivism, 6, 110–13
faithfulness, 77, 83, 116, 120, 125, 142–43, 145, 149
Federal Council of Churches, 33
fideism, 126–27
figural exegesis, 120–24
foundation(s), 116, 126, 128, 130
fundamentalism, 123
futurology, 125–26
generous orthodoxy, 33
gentiles, 65, 137–38, 140, 145–46

gospel, 7, 10–12, 14–15, 17, 21, 23, 28, 42, 69, 72, 103, 105, 128, 136
grace, 5, 10, 17–18, 42, 43, 45–46, 55, 63n24, 68, 71, 74–75, 92, 97–98, 100, 103, 106, 142, 148
habit(s), 45, 98, 118
halakhah, 18
(H)aggadah, 16, 18n61, 21n71
Hermeneutics, 9, 90, 117, 121–22,
historical-critical method, 32, 82, 122–24, 130n92
Holocaust, 148
indefectibility, 80n100
infallibility, 78–79, 80n100, 81, 84, 89–90
intratextuality, 116–17, 120–21, 125–26
Israel(ology), xi, 16n53, 65, 69, 77, 115, 120, 128, 133–153
Jews, Judaism, 13, 15–21, 23, 28, 65, 134n5, 137, 139–40, 141n34, 143, 145–52
justification, xi, 4, 11–12, 14, 20, 43, 70, 86, 90–106, 110
koinonia, 61, 71
laity, 66, 75–76
law, 14–15, 17–20, 77, 117, 123
liturgy (*leitourgia*), see worship
Lord's Prayer, 15, 19,
Lord's Supper (see Eucharist)

Index of Subjects

Lutheran-Catholic dialogue, x–xi, 80n100, 86, 91
Lutheran(ism), 1–24, 26, 36–37, 53–54, 57–60, 86, 91–106, 110, 131, 149
Lutheran World Federation, 57, 59–60
Marian dogmas, 41, 58, 82, 84, 114n31
mass, see Eucharist
Middle Ages, xi, 13, 26, 35, 39–56, 101, 106n72, 147
midrash, 16
mission, 2–4, 6, 61–63, 66–67, 85, 126–129, 143–44, 148, 153
narrative, 15–17, 21, 24, 50, 115, 122–24, 134–35, 137–39, 142, 145–46, 148 152,
National Council of Churches, 33
natural reason/theology, 45–46, 127–28
neo-orthodoxy, 26–27, 31
nouvelle théologie, 35–36, 122n66
observers (of the Second Vatican Council), x–xii, 2, 54–55, 57–59, 82–83, 86, 134, 152
Old Testament, 12, 20, 24, 121, 124n76, 137–39, 146
oneness of God, 46–51
papacy, 8, 30, 64n29, 73, 75–78, 110
Passover, 15, 16n52
Pelagianism, 42, 120

Petrine office, see papacy
philosophy, 21, 26, 31, 32n22, 34, 37, 39–41, 45, 54, 89, 98, 103, 127
pietism, 4–6, 123
postcritical, 124, 135
postliberal(ism), x–xi, 107–32
postmodernity, 30
prayer, 15, 19–20, 50, 68, 129, 145
preaching, 67–69, 72, 132
premodern exegesis, 122, 127, 130, 135
proofs for the existence of God, 26, 45–47, 90, 128
prophecy, prophets, 47, 65, 123, 125, 140, 149
rationality, rationalism, 45, 123, 127
reason, 41, 44–46, 51, 127–28
reconciliation, 71, 76, 78
 doctrinal reconciliation, 86–91, 106, 109–15
regula fidei, see rule of faith
relativism, 126
repentance, 149–50
ressourcement, 32–33, 36n39
Reformation, xi, 6–12, 14, 22–23, 36, 42, 45, 58, 65, 81, 95–96, 98, 100, 103–4, 122, 135, 142, 147
revelation, 41, 47, 78–79, 81, 128
Roman Catholicism, x–xi, 4–5, 7–8, 9n27, 11, 13, 22, 25–26, 28–29, 32, 34–37, 40–46, 51–52, 54–55, 57–101, 103, 105–6,

Index of Subjects

dogma(s) (*continued*)
    110–11, 114, 122n66,
    135–36, 147–48
romanticism, 123
rule of faith, 9, 115
rule theory of doctrine, 17,
    55, 101–6, 113–15
sacrament(s), 4, 15, 22, 46,
    63–64, 68–69, 71, 74,
    76, 87, 130, 136
salvation, 5, 10, 20, 43, 46, 62,
    64, 79, 95, 100–101,
    103, 106, 122, 144,
    149
scholasticism, 40, 63n24, 98,
    100
Second Vatican Council (see
    Vatican II)
sectarianism, 80
semi-Pelagianism, 42
service, 61, 66–68, 75
shema, 15, 143
sola fides, 10, 12, 43, 94, 103,
    105
sola gratia, 10, 12, 42, 100–1,
    142
sola scriptura, 10, 78, 80–81
solus Christus, 10
story (see narrative)
Student Christian Movement,
    35

supersessionism, 151
Talmud, 19
Tanakh, see Old Testament
Ten Commandments, 15,
    17–21
torah, see law
tradition, 10–12, 15, 17,
    21–23, 27, 30, 32, 40,
    44–45, 47, 52–53, 63,
    81, 83, 88–91, 93–94,
    100–101, 104, 108–
    11, 116, 120, 126–27,
    129–31, 141
transubstantiation, see
    Eucharist
Trinity, 46, 49, 51–54, 56
Vatican II, x–xii, 2, 37n46,
    54–55, 57–87, 90n20,
    134, 136, 152
witness, 10, 63, 65, 67–69, 71,
    73–75, 81, 134, 140,
    143–45, 151
works, 5, 14, 68n54, 69–70,
    74, 79, 92, 96, 98, 100,
    124, 151
World Council of Churches,
    33
Worship, 3, 14–15, 45, 50, 61,
    67–70, 74–75, 87, 99,
    140, 150–51
Yale, x, 25–27, 31–34, 37

www.ingramcontent.com/pod-product-compliance
Lightning Source LLC
Chambersburg PA
CBHW030112170426
43198CB00009B/589